SENSE AND SENSIBILITY
IN CHILDBIRTH

SENSE AND SENSIBILITY IN CHILDBIRTH

A Guide to Supportive Obstetrical Care

JUDITH HERZFELD, PH.D.

With original illustrations by Patricia Cobb

W · W · NORTON & COMPANY
New York · London

Published simultaneously in Canada by Penguin
Books Canada Ltd, 2801 John Street, Markham,
Ontario L3R 1B4.
The text of this book is composed in Times Roman, with
display type set in Palatino. Composition and
manufacturing by The Maple-Vail Book Manufacturing Group
Book design by Nancy Dale Muldoon

FIRST EDITION

Library of Congress Cataloging in Publication Data
Herzfeld, Judith.
Sense and sensibility in childbirth.
Bibliography: p.
Includes index.
1. Childbirth. 2. Obstetrics—Popular works.
1. Title
RG652.H38 1985   362.1'982   84–25564

ISBN 0-393-01983-7

W. W. Norton & Company, Inc., 500 Fifth Avenue, New York, N.Y. 10110
W. W. Norton Ltd., 37 Great Russell Street, London WC1B 3NU

1 2 3 4 5 6 7 8 9 0

To Sarah Rose and Rachel,
who light up my life.
It is my fond hope that by the time they are
old enough to understand what this book is about,
it will seem unfathomable that it ever had to be written.

CONTENTS

PREFACE

THIS book was written with the encouragement of friends who found my stories of negotiating my own obstetrical care interesting and my advice for negotiating their obstetrical care useful. Other than being a mother myself, my credentials for writing this book have nothing to do with obstetrics per se. Professionally I am a scientist engaged in teaching and research in a medical school department of physiology and biophysics. As a teacher, I am accustomed to predigesting and presenting technical information to more or less interested audiences. As a researcher, I am accustomed to taking a critical and quantitative view of the technical literature. As a colleague of physicians, but not being one myself, my views of medical care have the benefit of both some distance from the day-to-day fray and some access to the personalities and concerns of the participants.

Many people have contributed to this book knowingly and unknowingly. I am particularly grateful to Carol Griffin, Geri Denterlein, and Susan Burk for encouraging me to think that what I had to say was different enough and helpful enough to be worth taking the time to put in writing. The effort itself was inspired by Nancy Wainer Cohen's endless energy and commitment and Becky Sarah's special warmth and strength. Hilary Hinzmann buoyed the editing process with his enthusiasm for the book and his sensitivity to the issues it addresses. Along the way, helpful comments were also received from Constance Bean, Barbara Berger, Colleen Clark, Deborah Cline, Wayne Cohen, James

Courtemanche, Trudy Cox, Sophie Day, Lois Estner, Eugenia Marcus, Joan Mills, Kendrick Mills, Jane Pincus, Alice Rothchild, Jean Ryan, Beth Shearer, Sara Shields, Norma Shulman, Laura Sperazzi, and Norma Swenson.

Naturally, the personal influence of the obstetricians for my own pregnancies is especially strong. I would like to acknowledge the first for heightening my awareness of the controversies surrounding American childbirth by casting obstetrical issues in particularly high relief; the second for helping me consolidate my views by being willing to discuss the merits of various practices in an informed and open-minded fashion; and the third for providing the kind of care that should be the norm rather than the exception.

In my parents I have many causes to be grateful. Here I thank them especially for teaching me that reason and caring are most powerful when combined and that the only failure is not to have tried. Above all, I thank my husband for loving and sharing without confining.

ON LANGUAGE

WRITING from an unconventional perspective inevitably involves some struggle with language. Just as supportive obstetrical care is elusive in our culture, the language to describe it is also elusive. The word *deliver* is particularly problematic: to say that a woman delivers a baby is to cast her in a disinterested role of conveyor; to say that a doctor delivers a patient is to cast him in an exalted role of savior. Although there are times when an obstetrician needs to take an active role in birth, in most cases he need only observe and encourage while the mother brings forth her child herself. I prefer therefore to say that mothers birth their babies and obstetricians attend or assist them.

The natural-childbirth movement has generated some unfortunate vocabulary of its own. In particular, the designation of a *labor coach* suggests a need for instruction, coaxing, and exhortation in childbirth. However, what women really need most in labor is reassurance, encouragement, and creature comforts. In this book, the latter, more respectful form of help is distinguished from coaching by the use of the term *labor support* or *labor assistance*.

In some other matters of language I have felt it necessary to make concessions to convention. With apologies to all little girls, including my own, I have represented the babies in this book as male, to distinguish them more readily from their moms and to avoid jarring alternations in gender. Although I consider the healthy pregnant woman in the doctor's office and the healthy parturient in the hospital to be more suitably regarded as a client than a patient, I sometimes use the more common term in the interests of intelligibility. I also use male pronouns for doctors, because in reflecting what is still the usual situation it makes the text more readable. During the last five years, training programs in obstetrics and gynecology have increasingly included women. Although I am enthusiastic about this development for several reasons, the impact of these physicians on the practice of obstetrics in this country remains to be seen. Some of these women are content with the style of practice in which they have been trained and are not interested in change. Others who are committed to improvements have become discouraged about achieving significant change by working from the inside. In either case, it seems clear that, as in the past, the impetus for improvement has to come from the consumer.

I
Sense and Sensibility in Childbirth

1

CHOICE

A MOTHER-TO-BE is headed into new territory in many different respects. Not the least of these is the search for medical care for herself and her child. Chances are that she has never had to engage significant medical services before. Her medical needs up until this point have very likely been minimal, and any that may not have been were probably largely arranged for by her parents.

Obstetrics is a particularly problematic area in which to be an inexperienced consumer. To begin with, the stakes are high in that there are two patients in one; as a pair, mother and child are unusually vulnerable to physical, chemical, and psychological insults. In addition, decisions often have to be made under pressure of time, under physical stress, and under conditions which make it awkward, if not impossible, to obtain a second opinion. Finally, there is more difference of opinion and more rapidly changing opinion in obstetrics than in most medical specialties. The protocols of one hospital are ridiculed by others; what was considered outrageous five years ago is now standard practice.

By this time, it is widely accepted that natural childbirth (here taken to mean birth without drugs) is generally the healthiest childbirth. Unfortunately, however, supportive obstetrical care, which *encourages* natural childbirth and makes it most effective, is still the exception rather than the norm in American obstetrics. Several years ago I attended a memorable lecture on reasserting the role of instinct in childbirth. As we left the hall, I jokingly asked the woman nearest me how her birth experience had compared with the ones described in that talk. To my surprise, she enthusiastically responded, "Very well!" Then, she added more somberly, "But it took me three tries to get it that way." That simple remark expresses the experience of many American mothers. Typically, women attempting natural childbirth learn to work with their bodies and trust their instincts more with each successive birth. Looking back to their first birth experiences, they often feel that had they been encouraged to take this approach from the beginning, they and their babies would have been spared unnecessary difficulties. This book aims to provide that encouragement and to make the negotiation of supportive obstetrical care easier and more successful for the newcomer. It is dedicated to the premise that a woman should not have to learn about obstetrics by trial and error and that, given adequate information, each woman is the best judge of her own best interests and those of the child she nurtures.

In this age of planned parenthood, the need for obstetrical services can generally be anticipated well in advance. Unfortunately, however, options close more rapidly than most people realize. By the time pregnancy is established, it may be impossible to change to a health-care plan that is better suited to personal preferences. By the fifth or sixth prenatal office visit, a woman may find that she doesn't like her doctor or his partners as well as she had hoped. But she is probably six to seven months pregnant and reluctant to try to establish a working relationship with new practitioners. By the time most women start taking childbirth classes, they are well into the psychological "nesting" process of late pregnancy, which places a premium on feeling secure and well cared for often to the point of suppressing anxieties rather than dealing with them openly. Before the childbirth classes end, some members will already have given birth and the rest will follow shortly. Few, if any, will have exercised a serious choice in the care they receive, and the whole first pregnancy often turns out to be preparation for a real negotiation of care in subsequent pregnancies.

The lesson of this often-played scenario is that time is your most valuable asset and should not be allowed to slip through your fingers.

Your first priority, if it is still possible, should be to arrange health insurance that gives you as wide a range of choices of birth places and attendants as is within your means. After that, your most pressing need is to obtain independent information that will help you decide what kind of obstetrical care is right for you. This means learning about the physical and psychological aspects of childbirth and the procedures and technologies that are used by birth attendants. It does *not* mean worrying at this point about how to breathe through contractions or who gives the baby his first bath when. These are diversions from the really fundamental issues in childbirth. The ardor, effort, and concern elicited by these matters show how desperate parents are to lay some claim, however pathetic and nominal, to a process that has been largely taken from them. You don't have to settle for so little.

In obtaining information you should follow your common sense. There is no person or piece of writing (including this one and the ones recommended at the back of the book) that does not have its biases. No matter how authoritative the source, you should absorb what seems reasonable to you and set aside the rest. By consulting and comparing multiple sources, you are better able to judge what makes sense. You are also freed from those who would protect you from yourself. Some people won't tell you that human milk is the best food for your baby because they don't want you to feel guilty if you don't breast-feed. Others won't discuss the drawbacks of anesthesia for your labor and your baby because they don't want you to feel guilty if you do take pain relief. However, it is disrespectful and unethical for anyone to intervene between an adult woman and her conscience. There is no decision for which you should feel guilty if you have, in a fully informed manner and in the context of your personal situation, taken all the pros and cons into consideration.

Perhaps the most loaded word in childbirth today is *control*. Conventional methods of natural childbirth emphasize maternal control over the sensations of labor, and conventional approaches to obstetrics emphasize medical control over the progress of labor. However, efforts to control labor, whether by the mother or by the attendant, are highly problematic. In this respect, as in many others noted by various authors, childbirth is similar to intercourse. Active management frustrates both, and ultimately you have to let go and let it happen. Thus, when this book encourages maternal control in labor, it refers exclusively to the control of the *labor environment,* arranged as much as possible beforehand, that vests the mother with the trust and confidence to relinquish control of the *labor itself.* Human mothers, like animal mothers, benefit from a prepared birthing environment, free of disconcerting stimuli, unnecessary constraints, and excessive intrusion (or threat of intrusion).

Unfortunately, most women in our culture are socialized to take a relatively passive view of their environment.[1] As a result, they tend to focus on their own performance in a given situation, assuming that if they do well, everything else will fall into place. If their limited hopes are not fulfilled, they take the blame largely on their own shoulders. To the extent that women do not recognize the important influence of their environment, the chances of disappointed expectations are greater than they need be and the interpretation of disappointment in terms of personal failure is more devastating than it need be. Teamwork, in which the resources for success are multiplied and the blame for failure is divided, has been much less a part of the childhood experience of most women than of most men. Women are not accustomed to developing strategy and organizing their environment to given ends. As a consequence, they feel powerless to do anything but adapt themselves to the expectations and needs of others. Anything else seems foolhardy.

With regard specifically to childbirth, many women look at the practices in their community and suppress their misgivings about what they see. They feel bound to assume or hope that if they are diligent about their childbirth classes and ingratiating to their attendants, all will go well. Few appreciate that they can choose their team and coach it to play to their strengths. In fact, there is little in their experience to help them come to that appreciation or act upon it. The result is a sad state of affairs for all concerned. Not only are women not getting the care they want, but doctors are not getting the feedback they need. One professor of obstetrics laments that "perhaps the biggest problem for obstetricians has been to find out what kind of management in pregnancy women really want and what their expectations are . . . women almost never complain . . . even when their comments are invited . . . women do not risk offending the professionals in their own stronghold.''[2] Other progressive obstetricians say that women must communicate better with their physicians and insist on getting what they want. Actively negotiating obstetrical care can be challenging, but it is the most important step a mother can take for her child and herself. This book provides the information needed to motivate negotiating efforts and make them more effective.

The approach taken here is different in focus and organization from that of most books on childbirth. Some books provide encyclopedic coverage of the entire childbearing year, from the decision to conceive, to physical and social aspects of the postpartum period. This book concentrates instead on the several hours of that whole year which end the safest and closest association that mother and child will ever know. Because giving birth is a demanding process with a momentum all its own, childbirth is a particularly difficult time to exercise real choice about conduct with potentially overwhelming physical and psychological consequences. The attention needed to think through alternatives and the energy needed to communicate with attendants are likely to be preempted by the demands of the moment. The best way to avoid frustration and regrets is to think through alternatives in advance.

Even in regard to birth specifically, most books provide a catalogue of alternatives in the management of birth, with variously balanced views of the pros and cons of each individual option. Unfortunately, however, the smorgasbord in obstetrics is largely illusory because one or two choices can determine the rest of the menu. Although the better books do discuss the influence of each choice on others, the cumulative effect tends to be lost in a sea of detail. This book, in contrast, emphasizes the integrated effect and considers the individual options in terms of their contribution to the complete birth.

The book is divided into two parts. The first discusses the ingredients of supportive obstetrical care and how to justify these to attendants and friends who need to be convinced to help (or at least not hinder). In these chapters you will become familiar with the three categories of controversial obstetrical interventions, their roles in conventional management of birth, their implications for natural childbirth, and alternative approaches to the risks that they are meant to address. The discussion reflects the view that sense and sensibility are complimentary rather than antithetical, that reason should guide feelings and feelings should instruct reason.

The second part of the book develops a confidence-building strategy for obtaining supportive obstetrical services in our health-care system. Although it is primarily concerned with planning a hospital birth under the supervision of an obstetrician, it should also be useful to those making other arrangements. Supportive care has traditionally been the hallmark of the midwife and is often an interest of family-practice physicians. However, whether they work inside or outside the hospital, all responsible midwives and family practitioners will have provisions for obstetrical backup. These may involve restrictive rules for routine care, as well as inflexible protocols for the assessment and referral of complications. In general, such arrangements need to be evaluated at least as carefully as any made directly with an obstetrician. Whether your team is large or small, working in a hospital, a birthing center, or your home, the basis for organizing it and the strategies for success will be much the same.

Careful planning for your baby's birth will pay great dividends in the end. First and foremost, it will assure the healthiest possible outcome for you and your child. In addition, your contentment with the birth, self-esteem in mothering, and confidence in future dealings with physicians will all be enhanced. Incidentally, you will also contribute to the progress of obstetrical care. Each woman who works actively for responsive care makes that process easier for those who follow her.

2

FORM AND FUNCTION

THE first thing you should know about childbirth is that your body is more capable than you may realize and deserves more appreciation and cooperation from all concerned than is generally forthcoming. In order to defend this point of view in discussions with others, you need to have some familiarity with normal reproductive anatomy (form) and physiology (function).

PELVIC RELATIONSHIPS

The uterus in which your baby grows is a muscular pouch positioned somewhat like an inverted bottle at the inner end of the vagina. The top (if you are standing up) is called the fundus, the neck at the bottom is called the cervix, and the flaring-out region above the neck is called the lower segment. As your baby grows, the uterus enlarges upward into the abdomen, so that one measure of the progress of gestation is the so-called "height of the fundus" relative to more stationary anatomical features such as your pubic bone, your navel, and your rib cage.

The uterus sits nestled in a funnel-like ring of bones called the pelvis, with the bladder in front and the rectum behind. The wide top of the funnel (known as the "false pelvis") is formed by the ilia (the bones you feel when you put your hands on your hips). The narrow bottom of the funnel (known as the "true pelvis") is a curved passage bounded in front by the pubis (the bones felt under the pubic hair), on each side by the ischia (the bones that support your weight when you sit up straight), and in back by the sacrum and coccyx (the tailbones). The narrowest part of the pelvis is at the level of the ischial spines. These are two small projections from the inner surface of the ischia, behind the socket of the hip joint, which point toward the tip of the coccyx. The position of the top of the baby's head during labor is measured relative to these prominences, in negative centimeters above and positive centimeters below. Coming through the pelvis are the urethra in front, which empties the bladder, the rectum in back, which empties the intestines, and the vagina in the middle, which, to put it most unromantically, receives the sperm and empties the uterus of the products of conception: the baby, the amniotic sac with placenta, and the cord connecting the two.

Compared to the male version, the female pelvis's open structure is clearly designed to allow a baby's passage. The dimensions of the pelvic outlet can be estimated by manual examination and with x-rays, but these procedures (called pelvimetry) do not reliably predict the ease or difficulty of birth. This is only partly due to the inherent imprecision of the methods. The size of the baby's head, the direction it faces, and the extent to which it molds to the shape of the pelvis all affect the birth process. In addition, the cartilage between the pelvic bones softens under the influence of relaxin (a hormone produced by the uterus and placenta late in pregnancy and during labor). This renders the pelvis more flexible than normal and thus more responsive to expulsive forces and maternal position. Given these many variables, the exposure of the ovaries and the baby to x-rays for pelvimetry is falling into disrepute. Unless there is obvious pelvic deformity (due to childhood disease or malnutrition) or the baby is not presenting head first, the best test of proportion between the mother's pelvis and the baby's head is a good "trial of labor."

From the bones of the pelvis, the pelvic organs are supported by a multilayered hammock of ligaments and muscles known collectively as the "pelvic floor." The muscles are probably most familiar to you from their use to control urination and defecation. However, you also use them, reflexively if not consciously, in sexual intercourse. Tension in the pelvic floor can impede the passage of a baby, just as it impedes the passage of urine or feces. Relaxation, on the other hand, helps the muscles stretch around the baby as it is born. For several decades, American obstetricians argued that cutting the muscles (episiotomy) was better for the subsequent integrity of the pelvic floor than stretching. However, in order to minimize blood loss and pain, episiotomy is not normally done until the muscle is already stretched very thin. In any case, episiotomy has not been proven effective in preventing weakness of the pelvic floor in later life.[1] As with any other set of muscles, the best method for improving and maintaining the condition of the pelvic floor is exercise. Exercises specifically for these muscles are called Kegel exercises.

THE ONSET OF LABOR

During pregnancy, the cervix or neck of the uterus is normally firm and long, with a narrow opening, the os, that is plugged with mucus. At the end of gestation, the cervix becomes soft and short, as the cervical canal is gradually drawn open (taken up), first at the inner end (effacement or thinning) and then at the outer end (dilatation or dilation). The factors determining the onset of labor in humans are subtler than in other species and not thoroughly understood. In general, bodily functions are controlled by electrical signals (nerve impulses) and chemical messages (hormones and related molecules). However, because many different things are going on at once, because very small changes in electrical or chemical activity can have large effects, and because the definitive experiments cannot ethically be done on humans, it is often difficult to tease apart cause and effect. In pregnancy this becomes even more complicated because the fetus's own developing neuroendocrine (nerve and hormone) system contributes to the overall neuroendocrine status of the mother-child pair. In fact, one of the few things that can

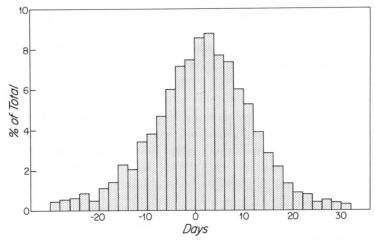

FIGURE 1. THE LENGTH OF GESTATION

Percentage of births in two-day intervals before and after the conventional due date. The distribution is broad and peaks after the due date. *(After Page[3])*

be said with confidence about the onset of labor is that it normally waits for a "ready" signal from the baby's neuroendocrine system.[2]

In terms of the safe development of the infant, the primary concern of the neuroendocrine system must be to prevent labor from starting too soon. The muscular wall of the uterus is designed to contract, and the estrogen produced by the fetus and the placenta during pregnancy stimulates both the growth and the contractile ability of the uterus. Progesterone, which is produced early in pregnancy by the ovary and later in pregnancy by the placenta, reinforces the growth effects of estrogen while suppressing regular contractions until gestation is complete. The opposing effects of these two hormones on uterine muscle activity seem to be related to their opposing effects on prostaglandin synthesis. Prostaglandins act to induce cervical ripening (the softening and thinning of the cervix) and uterine contractions (as in menstrual cramps). Estrogen stimulates prostaglandin production, and progesterone inhibits it.

The coordinated uterine contractions of labor develop as prostaglandin levels rise. It is not yet known exactly how the fetus triggers this increase, although fetal secretion of oxytocin has been implicated in the process.[4] Once begun, prostaglandin release and uterine contractions stimulate each other in a positive feedback manner, so that the intensity and frequency of contractions progressively increase. In this manner, the baby normally precipitates the events leading to his semi-independent existence when he is ready.

Other biochemical developments at term seem to complement those that initiate and sustain labor. The high estrogen levels characteristic of late pregnancy have been observed (in experiments with animals) to stimulate maternal behavior.[5] The rise in endorphins (the body's own opiates) prior to and during birth[6] has been associated (also in experiments with animals) with an elevated pain threshhold[7] and their decline after birth with enhanced maternal expression.[8] Interestingly, the latter effect was disrupted by treatment with botanical opiates used for pain medication. The influences of estrogen and endorphins diminish rapidly after birth. In the animals studied, the pain threshold dropped sharply postpartum, temporarily dipping below normal in the second week, and sustained maternal behavior depended on early postpartum ("after parting") interaction with the offspring. Estrogen and endorphin levels may have similar psychological importance in humans. This could explain the special value of early mother-infant interaction for bonding and the lower tolerance for pain in induced labors and in recovery from surgical birth.

THE FIRST STAGE OF LABOR

Labor proceeds in several stages. During the first stage, the muscle fibers in the upper portion of the uterus shorten with each contraction, pulling on the lower portion. By this means the lower segment is stretched thin and the cervix is retracted around the baby so that the opening is dilated. The boundary between the upper, active portion of the uterus and the lower, passive part is known as the retraction ring, and its upward progress can be followed by palpating the abdomen.[9] This process is important even in cesarean birth. Abdominal delivery late in labor, through a horizontal incision in a well-thinned lower segment, does less damage to the uterus (as judged by an at least tenfold lower frequency of subsequent uterine "rupture") than early in labor, through a similar incision in an incompletely thinned lower segment.[10]

The first stage of labor generally proceeds most quickly and comfortably if the woman is relaxed and walking about. Movement in general helps, and, in the upright position, contractions are more effective though less frequent.[11] Lying on the back is the worst position for labor. In this position, the weight of the uterus compresses the major blood vessels behind it and impairs blood circulation.[12] A raised backrest only partially corrects the problem. When bedrest seems desirable during labor, or generally in late pregnancy, lying on the side is preferable.

The first stage of labor may be divided into three phases: the latent phase, the active phase, and the transition phase. During the latent phase, the contractions are usually mild and well spaced, and the dilation of the cervix is relatively slow. In this phase, environmental disturbances (such as loss of privacy or uncomfortable examination) often cause contractions to stop. Typically, at about four centimeters dilation, the contractions become noticeably stronger, more closely spaced, and more strongly established. This is known as active labor, and its intense traction on the lower part of the uterus usually brings about more rapid dilation. This part of labor is thus more demanding but also more promising. Environmental disturbances during this phase are less likely to affect progress but may increase pain. As full dilation approaches (ten centimeters), the nature of the contractions begins to change to those of the second stage. This nebulous period is known as the transition phase. It may be a confusing and intense time for the mother, calling for sensitivity and encouragement on the part of attendants.

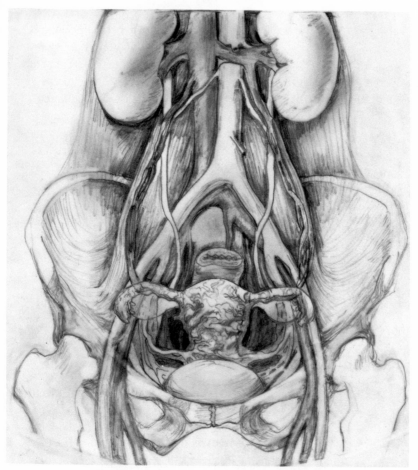

FIGURE 2. BLOOD VESSELS SUPPLYING THE PELVIS

The uterus (here shown nonpregnant) sits nestled in the pelvis with the bladder in front and the rectum (here shown truncated) behind. The arteries (light) supplying blood to the area and the veins (dark) returning blood to the heart run along the back, between the kidneys. In late pregnancy the enlarged uterus compresses these blood vessels when the mother lies on her back. This hinders the circulation generally and blood flow to the uterus in particular. *(Patricia Cobb, after Tom Jones*[13]*)*

15

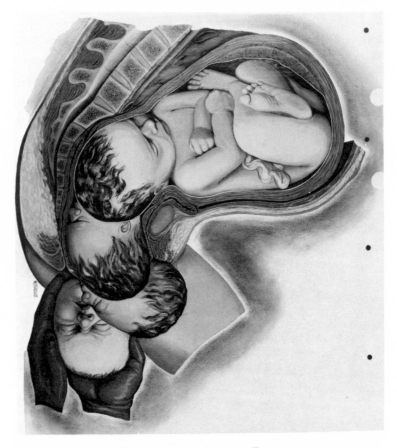

FIGURE 3. GRAVITY ASSISTING EXPULSION

Movement of the baby through the curved birth canal is facilitated by various upright postures (here kneeling) that take advantage of gravity. *(Margaret Gamper, R.N., originator; Nelle I. Bartusch, designer and artist)*

THE SECOND STAGE OF LABOR

In the second stage of labor, the uterus pushes the baby down. Once the second-stage character of the contractions is well developed, an undrugged mother will spontaneously begin to bear down. This extra

16

expulsive effort by the respiratory muscles helps to push the baby out. However, if overdone it can significantly impair the oxygen supply to the uterus and the baby. Spontaneous short pushes are less fatiguing, and put less stress on the baby and on the mother's tissues, than strained long pushes.[14]

Typically, the second stage proceeds with least effort if the mother is upright: squatting, kneeling, or standing with or without various supports. Her bottom should be relaxed: open without being overstretched by spreading the legs more than is comfortable. The vaginal tissues, which soften and expand during late pregnancy, readily accommodate the approximately four-inch diameter of the baby's head. As the baby progresses downward, the area around the vaginal opening bulges and stretches. Because of the curvature of the birth canal, the bulging and stretching are greatest in the perineum, the tissue between the vagina and the rectum. The common delivery positions in industrial societies (bottom tipped up to give the attendant access to the perineum) increase the pressure on the perineum, and thereby increase the risk of tearing it. If it is not possible to maintain an upright position to distribute the pressure of the baby's head more evenly, then the Sims position (lying on the left side with the right leg supported by an assistant) should be considered. Ceasing to bear down when stretching sensations are felt so that the baby is eased out gently will also minimize tearing.

In the question of position, as in other matters, it is important to distinguish between cultural and biological imperatives. Although many aspects of childbirth vary from one culture to another, there is no nonindustrial society (among the hundreds which have been studied) in which women give birth on their backs with their feet in the air, as on an American delivery table. In 50 percent of the nonindustrial societies, women squat or kneel for birth; in 20 percent, they sit or stand; in 30 percent, they are partially or fully reclining; and in a small number they are on hands and knees.[15] Other primates in the second stage of birth adopt the position they use for defecation, and human beings do well to do likewise (with the caveat that the Western-style toilet is higher than is optimal for either defecation or birth). The torso-upright positions not

17

only facilitate birth, they also allow more direct first interactions with the baby, particularly the eye contact that mothers and newborns seek.

THE THIRD STAGE OF LABOR

The third stage of labor begins after the baby is born. Uterine contractions shear the placenta from the uterine wall, and bleeding at the placental site leads to the formation of the retroplacental clot. Further contractions then act simultaneously to close off the maternal blood vessels that fed the baby, via the placenta and umbilical cord, and to push out the placenta. It is not necessary to clamp or cut the cord at this time or ever. Valves in the blood vessels prevent fetal blood from being lost, and the cord will dry up and fall off whether still attached to the placenta or not. While it is admittedly more convenient to separate the baby from the placenta before nature does so, there is no justification for routinely clamping the cord before it has stopped pulsing and the baby has received his entitlement of blood.[16] Indeed, it appears that the placenta is more readily loosened and expelled from the uterus if it is allowed to empty.[17] Expulsion of the placenta is also facilitated by an upright posture that takes advantage of gravity. Timely completion of the third stage is critical for the mother's safety. If the uterus does not contract efficiently, hemorrhage and infection may occur through the open blood vessels. If the labor has been unusually difficult due to anatomical or psychophysiological resistance, the uterus may be too exhausted to contract spontaneously and stimulation (manual and pharmacological) may be required.

THE DURATION OF LABOR

A course of labor is illustrated in Figure 4, using the kind of graph often used by obstetricians.[18] Although the pattern is representative, the time over which a perfectly normal labor might stretch is highly variable. Our cultural view is generally that the faster a job can be done,

18

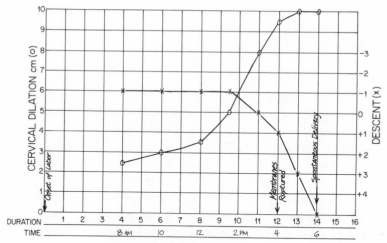

FIGURE 4. THE FRIEDMAN CURVE

The duration of labor is highly variable, but the pattern shown here is typical: gentle labor with slow dilation, followed by vigorous labor with rapid dilation, and, finally, pushing with descent of the baby.

the better, and that every effort should be made to conform to a standard of no-nonsense efficiency. The issue of time will be discussed in detail in Chapter 6. In general, precipitate (very short) labors, whether spontaneous or induced, are associated with less-than-optimal outcomes for both mother and baby. On the other hand, when problematic outcomes are associated with long labors, they are generally the result of factors (sometimes aggravated by the attendants) that have nothing to do with time per se.[19]

If we compare the physical activity of birth with that of climbing a mountain, it becomes obvious that a mad dash to the finish may leave the participants in considerably worse shape than a steady, moderate pace tailored to the capacities of the participants. In childbirth, the blood supply to the uterus is shut off at the peak of each contraction. In normal active labor, without vigorous pushing, this deprivation occurs for a tolerable fifteen to twenty seconds every three minutes. However, if the contractions are abnormally long, strong, or frequent, as is common with the aggressive use of labor stimulants, your uterus and your baby are forced to hold their breath for longer periods with shorter intervals for recovery. Although this is tolerable to a point because of nature's built-in reserve, the extra stress is unnecessary and imprudent. Certainly it is not something that most of us would choose to subject our babies to after they are born, or indeed choose for ourselves.

The accepted drugs for induction or stimulation of labor are oxytocin and prostaglandins. The more commonly used agent, oxytocin (which often goes by the brand names Pitocin and Syntocinon), affects only uterine contractions, while prostaglandins promote cervical ripening as well. Thus, oxytocin is useful only if the cervix is already soft. On the other hand, prostaglandins (alone or with small amounts of oxytocin)[20] have been used to induce parturition in humans at all stages of gestation, and it is widely thought that increased prostaglandin production is reponsible for premature labor in women with intrauterine infections, hemorrhage, overdistension of the uterus, ruptured membranes and systemic disease. Whatever the exact role of prostaglandins may be, drugs that inhibit prostaglandin synthesis are often able to suppress premature labor.

The natural production of oxytocin and prostaglandins in normal labor is subject to strong internal controls that cannot be duplicated in external administration. In fact, neither maternal nor infused oxytocin is necessary for labor to proceed. Maternal oxytocin normally becomes important only at the end of the second stage, when it facilitates third-stage clamping of uterine blood vessels and postpartum milk letdown. Increased maternal oxytocin secretion at this time is provoked by the distension of the birth canal during the baby's passage,[21] a reflex that is suppressed by nerve-blocking anesthesia.[22]

Although maternal oxytocin is not necessary for labor to proceed, it can make a difference. Natural oxytocin production can be increased by sexual stimulation. This effect is particularly obvious postpartum, in

20

milk letdown during intercourse. The oxytocin-promoting effect of sexual activity, in addition to the presence of prostaglandins in semen and the prostaglandin-stimulating activity of bacteria, has caused physicians to proscribe intercourse in unstable pregnancies in order to minimize the chances of premature labor. By the same logic, it would seem appropriate to prescribe sexual activity in post-date pregnancies in order to encourage the onset of labor. In traditional societies, sexual arousal and orgasm are recognized means of stimulating labor. In this country, sexual stimulation of labor is encouraged by very few attendants. However, breast stimulation is now sometimes used instead of intravenous oxytocin to induce uterine contractions in the prenatal fetal stress test.[23] It has also been used to induce cervical ripening and spontaneous labor after thirty-nine weeks' gestation.[24]

Natural oxytocin production can be depressed by anxiety, an effect that is also particularly obvious after birth, in the inhibition of milk letdown during breast feeding. It so happens that anxiety also stimulates the release of catecholamines. These chemicals make the uterus relax; at the same time, they make blood vessels constrict in all the tissues, including the uterus, that are not essential to the "fight or flight" response of a frightened animal. The combined effect of depressed oxytocin and elevated catecholamines can strongly inhibit labor.

As discussed earlier, the role of the fetus in initiating labor is well recognized even though it is not well understood. It is also known that the fetus, like his mother, produces "fight or flight" hormones when stressed by food or oxygen deprivation.[25] However, the possibility that a distressed fetus may thereby be able to slow down labor to his own benefit has so far been ignored. Under these circumstances, pushing the labor with drugs would produce full-blown fetal distress. On the other hand, improving the baby's environment would relieve his stress and allow labor to proceed. Walking when possible and lying on the side when resting improve blood circulation to the fetus. Nourishment also helps to prevent a fetal "fight or flight" response. In our present state of ignorance regarding the degree to which the fetus can tailor labor to his needs, we should be very cautious about overriding natural control mechanisms.

A CAPABLE BODY

The following chapters will discuss many factors that influence childbirth. However, a discussion of reproductive anatomy and physiology would not be complete without emphasizing the importance of good nutrition. Pregnancy is a time of astounding growth. Not only is a new human being developing, but the placenta, uterus, and blood supply are also growing. A uterus without the resources to develop well will not be able to contain the pregnancy to term or expel it properly at term. A placenta without the resources to develop well will not be able to exchange nutrients and wastes adequately or secrete hormones properly throughout pregnancy and labor. Water retention increases automatically in pregnancy in order to form the extra blood needed to serve the uterus and the baby. But if the resources to form blood proteins are not available, the retained water will simply leak into the tissues and cause excessive swelling.

The body's ability to compensate for nutritional inadequacy is limited. When a pregnant woman's blood volume is low, her body tries to adjust by pumping the available blood faster. As the needs of the uterus, placenta, and fetus increase during pregnancy, this mechanism can lead progressively to skyrocketing blood pressure, kidney damage with leakage of blood proteins into the urine (aggravating the original protein shortage), bleeding into the liver and brain, convulsions and coma (eclampsia), and death. This process, known as toxemia, is one of the most serious complications of pregnancy and one of the greatest causes of maternal death. Although the disease involves water accumulation in the tissues (pitting edema), the problem is exacerbated by water pills (diuretics) and dietary salt restriction because they further reduce blood volume. If damage to the liver and the kidneys is not too great, initiation of a high-protein diet can promote the accumulation of blood proteins needed to keep water in the circulation and expand blood volume.[26]

Otherwise, the only known means of improving the situation is carefully controlled infusion of blood proteins directly into the circulation.[27]

Other pregnancy complications attributable to malnutrition are poor fetal development, premature separation of the placenta, premature birth, and difficult labor.[28] Premature separation of the placenta (known medically as *abruptio placentae*) detaches the baby's *in utero* lifeline and leaves the mother hemorrhaging into the uterus. Poor fetal development, premature birth, and difficult labor are associated with increased birth defects, particularly brain damage. Although the consequences of marginally inadequate nutrition are less dramatic, good nutrition remains important for an optimal outcome for mother and child.

The resources available for your pregnancy are influenced by many substances besides foods. For example, inhaled carbon monoxide, a product of the incomplete combustion of such organic materials as tobacco, combines with the hemoglobin in your blood to make less of it available for transporting oxygen to the uterus and placenta. Other chemicals, such as nicotine, alcohol, caffeine, drugs (over-the-counter, prescription, and recreational), pollutants (of the general environment, the workplace, and the home), and food additives, pass through the placenta into the fetal circulation before they are completely removed by the mother's liver. In addition to their direct effects (known and unknown) on mother and child,[29] these substances put an extra load on the mother's liver that can affect its ability to produce the proteins needed to expand her blood supply and remove the hormones that are generated by the placenta (about one hundred contraceptive pills' worth per day). In general, any drug or other chemical that is not providing a clear and compelling benefit for which there is no acceptable alternative should be avoided. Necessary medication should be taken in the lowest dose and with the lowest frequency that is effective. This is especially so during labor because, once born, the infant is entirely dependent on his own relatively immature liver to clear his blood of drugs. Any drugs remaining in the circulation at birth will be removed much more slowly from the infant's body than from the mother's body.

It is because pregnancy and birth are strenuous undertakings that they are relatively unforgiving of poor health habits. On the other hand, there is no other strenuous activity for which your body is better designed (or more richly rewarded). If you are healthy and take good care of yourself, you can confidently expect that you and your baby will thrive in pregnancy and work effectively through labor and birth.

3

ALL OR NONE

MEDICAL advances allow us to approach childbirth without fear of eventualities that struck terror into the hearts of our grandmothers. The decline in maternal mortality in this century is largely the result of early delivery to resolve toxemia, fibrinogen and blood transfusions to treat hemorrhage, and antibiotics to fight infection. In addition, advances in neonatology have improved the chances of survival and the quality of life of premature infants. Although some toxemia, hemorrhage, infection, and prematurity have been iatrogenic (physician-caused), and the availability of solutions to these problems has allowed irresponsible doctors to be sloppy, the fact remains that medical resources are important to maternal and infant well-being. Nature can be wasteful of things we consider precious; and, whatever its faults, when there is a clear and present need for intervention, medicine does quite well. On the other hand, most women with good prenatal care are well equipped to give birth to a healthy baby without any medical attention. In general, it is hard to improve on the natural process and easy to do worse.

Although it is not difficult to identify potential problems in obstetrics, it is difficult indeed to show that a proposed solution really improves matters. In fact, none of the *routine* interventions in childbirth has been shown to improve outcomes for either mothers or babies, and it is becoming increasingly evident that their indiscriminate use creates at least as many problems as it solves. The controversial practices in obstetrics can be grouped into three categories: prophylaxis, pain medication, and medical delivery. Prophylaxis includes those practices, such as electronic monitoring, fasting, IV, and episiotomy, that are meant to prevent potential problems. The purpose of fetal monitoring is to detect fetal asphyxia, *should* it occur, early enough to be able to avoid damage to the baby. The purpose of fasting is to prevent the aspiration of stomach contents under anesthesia, *should* anesthesia become necessary. The purpose of an intravenous line is to provide a direct route for drugs, blood, and fluids, *should* an emergency develop, as well as to forestall dehydration while fasting. The purpose of episiotomy is to prevent tearing the perineum, *should* it not stretch enough. Pain medication includes both analgesia, to "take the edge off," and anesthesia to remove sensation. Medical delivery includes the artificial rupture of membranes or the administration of drugs to stimulate contractions, episiotomy to expedite delivery by reducing the time taken to stretch the perineum, forceps or suction to pull the baby's head through the vagina, and cesarean delivery to circumvent passage through the pelvis.

These three categories of practices are strongly connected. The interrelationships are represented by the triangle shown in Figure 5. Pain medication increases the need for prophylaxis and medical delivery, prophylaxis increases the need for pain medication and medical delivery, and medical delivery increases the need for pain medication and prophylaxis. The effect is a kind of all-or-none phenomenon. Once you accept one of these practices, it becomes more likely that you will get all three. For women who fear labor or lack adequately supportive attendants, it starts with pain medication. For others, it starts with electronic monitoring, fasting, and / or labor stimulants. In either case, the result is often the full triumvirate in one form or the other. The bottom line is that either you keep your body unencumbered and birth your baby the way nature intended, or he will very likely have to be extracted. In between is quicksand.

In case this seems very abstract and philosophical to you, let me try to make it more concrete. At North Central Bronx Hospital in New

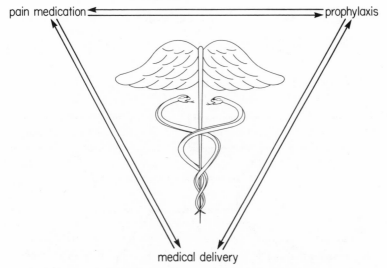

pain medication ◄─────────────────────────────► prophylaxis

medical delivery

FIGURE 5. THE TRIANGLE OF CONVENTIONAL OBSTETRICS

Obstetrical practices can be categorized according to their intent to suppress pain, prevent potential complications, and expedite delivery. Each type of practice increases the need for the others.

York City, all births, including the large proportion of high-risk cases (30 percent), are attended by midwives with a backup obstetrician on call for complications. In this service the use of pain medication and prophylaxis is very low, and in 1979 good infant outcomes were obtained with a rate of spontaneous vaginal birth of 88.5 percent. Cesarean delivery accounted for 9 percent of births (7 percent primary and 2 percent repeat), and instrumental delivery (forceps and suction) accounted for the remaining 2.5 percent. Supportive care is also emphasized at Booth Maternity Center in Philadelphia. There, too, a relatively high-risk patient population (30 percent at medical risk) receives care from nurse-midwives with in-house obstetrical backup. Referring only the 2.5 percent of their cases with major medical problems (such as kidney or heart

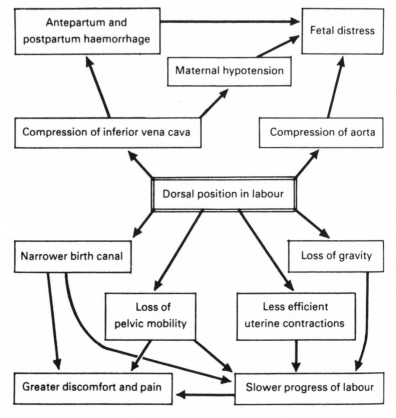

FIGURE 6. CONSEQUENCES OF THE DORSAL POSITION

A detailed example of the general relationships shown in Figure 5: the dorsal position, which is especially encouraged in fetal monitoring, increases the need for pain medication and medical delivery. *(From* The Lancet,[1] *with permission)*

failure, premature delivery, or insulin-dependent diabetes) to a tertiary-level center, the rate of spontaneous vaginal birth at Booth in 1980 was 88.2 percent. Cesarean delivery occurred in 7.8 percent of cases (5.6 percent primary and 2.2 percent repeat), and forceps were used in the remaining 4 percent. At Beth Israel Hospital in Boston, on the other hand, prophylaxis is routine and pain medication is used more freely. There, in 1976 and 1981, the rates of spontaneous vaginal birth were 63 percent and 65 percent, respectively. Cesarean delivery accounted for 21 percent of births in 1976 and 20 percent of births (14 percent primary and 6 percent repeat) in 1981. In spite of the relatively strong commitment of this service to minimizing intervention in the second stage of labor, instrumental delivery accounted for 16 percent of births in 1976 and 15 percent of births in 1981. Most other hospitals do much worse. Forceps rates over 40 percent are not unusual.

What does this mean for you? If your baby is one of those who, as one doctor put it, "practically falls out," you'll have a spontaneous vaginal birth in any case, although unnecessary prophylaxis and pain medication will increase the chances of needing a little assistance in the form of labor stimulation and episiotomy. However, if your situation turns out to be one of the ones that needs more work, unnecessary prophylaxis and pain medication may make the difference between a spontaneous vaginal birth and an instrumental or cesarean delivery. Putting it another way, if you recently had a cesarean delivery in the average American obstetrical practice, the chances are greater than 50 percent that it could have been avoided without adverse consequences (by the kind of care given at the North Central Bronx Hospital and the Booth Maternity Center). If you recently had an instrumental delivery in the average American obstetrical practice, the chances are greater than 80 percent that it could have been avoided without untoward effect.

Now you may ask, "What is so bad about a medical delivery that I should care so much about avoiding it?" Part of the problem is psychological. Women are often surprised by the indelibility of their childbirth experience and the lasting importance attached to matters that would otherwise seem inconsequential. However, we know that memory is generally unusually sharp around occasions of great emotional significance (aptly called memorable events). To the extent that a woman has a strong emotional involvement in her child's birth, she is likely to be lastingly impressed by the incidents surrounding it.

Unfortunately, some women feel, consciously or subconsciously, that a medical delivery reflects negatively on their competence or femininity. In fact, studies have found that a woman's satisfaction with childbirth is strongly related to her sense of autonomy and mastery.[2] Others feel that something is left incomplete or unresolved in a medical delivery, that medical delivery disrupts a psychological transition that should accompany the baby's physical passage from intrauterine to extrauterine life. Childbirth may be experienced as an occasion for personal growth or as an unavoidable affliction. Clearly, medical delivery serves better as a cure of an affliction than as a basis for growth. Often, colloquial expressions convey feelings that medical terminology avoids. For example, when labor and delivery personnel say that a doctor who is infusing Pitocin to stimulate labor is "pitting" his patient, they express the potential insidiousness of being connected to a pump that, at the twist of someone else's impatient wrist, can take over your body and throw you and your baby into hard labor.

Whatever the psychological repercussions, it is clear that medical deliveries can cause unnecessary physical trauma to mother and baby.

(1) Surgical rupture of the amniotic sac (accomplished by inserting a crochetlike hook through a partially dilated cervix) can sometimes strengthen labor. This is thought to occur because the broken membranes release precursors of prostaglandins, because distension of the vagina by the operator's hand may stimulate oxytocin secretion, or because the baby's head directly applied to the cervix exerts more pressure than the amniotic fluid. However, by removing the fluid cushion, rupture of the membranes (referred to medically as ROM) also increases the pressure on the baby's head. In addition, if the baby's head is not already well applied to the cervix, rupturing the membranes may cause the umbilical cord (which normally floats on the amniotic fluid) to drop past the baby's head (prolapse) and become pinched when the baby descends. A prolapsed cord is life-threatening for the baby and requires a cesarean delivery. Even when there is no prolapse, amniotic fluid seems to protect the cord from compression.[3]

Rupturing the membranes also opens a pathway for infection that cannot be allowed to remain open indefinitely. If ROM is not effective in stimulating labor, oxytocin will have to be used. If oxytocin does not bring about birth in a timely fashion, a cesarean delivery will be necessary. A mother with ruptured membranes works against the clock and often loses. When ROM is effective in stimulating labor, the change in the pattern of contractions may be abrupt and difficult to adjust to, increasing the need for pain medication. Membranes may inadvertently rupture before full dilation, either naturally (about 20 percent of the time) or in the course of examination. But this does not recommend ROM. The intact membranes' extra protection against fetal distress may make the difference between a vaginal and a cesarean delivery in the end. The extra protection against infection may make the difference between an easy and a complicated postpartum course.

(2) The use of oxytocin to stimulate labor has already been discussed in the previous chapter. Oxytocic drugs do not produce a normal active labor. Even if the drug is chemically indistinguishable from the oxytocin your body generates, it is introduced in a manner totally different from the way your body would produce it. It is infused in greater-than-normal amounts, without feedback control and without complementation by the other biochemicals (known and unknown) involved in normal labor. The result, especially in sustained aggressive use, is abnormal water retention and abnormally long and strong contractions, with shorter intervals for recovery and greater need for pain medication.

Because of the hypersensitivity of some women to oxytocin, the drug *must* be introduced in a carefully controlled manner. This requires an intravenous infusion and all that goes with it (see Chapter 5). Since it takes about forty minutes for a particular infusion rate to reach its maximum effectiveness, the dose *must* be adjusted very slowly, starting at the lowest setting.[4] Because of the potential for fetal distress and uterine rupture, electronic monitoring *must* be used. If fetal distress develops, the oxytocin will have to be turned off and oxygen will need to be administered. If the baby's condition does not improve, there will be an emergency cesarean delivery. However, some damage to the baby may already have occurred by this time. Even when fetal distress is not recorded, some mothers feel that their babies have been more high-

31

strung and difficult to comfort when oxytocin has been used to shorten the first stage of labor. In addition, the use of oxytocin is associated with a higher incidence of postpartum hemorrhage.

(3) Episiotomy was formerly recommended in this country to prevent prolapse of pelvic organs into the vagina later in life. The assumption was that cutting and stitching weakened the muscles of the pelvic floor less than stretching. However, the efficacy of episiotomy in this regard has never been proven, and episiotomy for this purpose has fallen into disrepute. Routine episiotomy was also recommended to spare the baby's head the supposed hardship of being "pounded" against the mother's perineum. However, there is no evidence that stretching the perineum poses any difficulty for the baby. This is especially so if the mother relaxes her pelvic floor and assumes a position that distributes the pressure evenly. In any case, the time spent stretching the perineum is far less than that spent stretching the cervix; it makes more sense to protect the baby's head by keeping the amniotic membranes intact as long as possible in the first stage than by cutting the perineum in the second stage. At this time, the usual rationale for an episiotomy is to prevent tearing the perineum. However, progressive obstetricians agree that few mothers will tear enough in a spontaneous birth to be better off with an episiotomy. An episiotomy may also be done to shorten the second stage of labor, with or without forceps. Some obstetricians even do episiotomies to facilitate delivery of the baby's shoulders, although repositioning the mother is a more effective way of dealing with shoulder dystocia.

Depending upon the practitioner and the situation, the cut may be major or minor, may extend (tear beyond the original cut), and may be repaired with more or less skill. In closing the wound, failure to match the two sides of the incision properly is a particular concern. A 1980 review of operative intervention in childbirth states, "The episiotomy repair should include re-approximation of the incised tissues anatomically. Although this basic principle should need no explanation, it is emphasized here because it is often overlooked."[5] Episiotomy is also associated with a substantial increase in infection.[6]

There are two types of episiotomy. The midline episiotomy, cut in the direction of the anus, is made in the same place where natural tears tend to occur. However, the cut itself is deeper than most tears, and further tearing of the weakened perineum may occur as far as the anus. In fact, the worst tears in obstetrics tend to be extensions of episiotomies. The mediolateral episiotomy, which is cut obliquely toward one leg or the other, is less likely to extend or involve the anus. But this episiotomy cuts into thicker muscle, causes considerably more pain postpartum, and heals relatively slowly. A study of 1,800 women in England, where episiotomies are usually mediolateral, found that "women who had episiotomies were more likely to have pain at the end of the first week after birth and to experience pain with intercourse for longer than two months than those who had *large* tears" (emphasis added).[7] The chief of obstetrics at one of Harvard's major teaching hospitals says flatly that "if a woman does not want an episiotomy she shouldn't have one."

(4) Everyone knows that forceps can cause trauma to the baby's head. Squeezing a little too tightly or pulling a little too hard can cause devastating brain damage.[8] In addition, tension applied to the baby's head can stress the neck and traumatize the upper end of the spinal cord.[9] Such damage has been associated with stillbirth and neonatal death. Forceps may also cause injury to nerves of the face, shoulders, and arms, as well as fracture of the collar bone.[10] Because of these factors and subtler effects, and because of improvements in the safety of the cesarean alternative, high-forceps extractions are no longer done by responsible attendants and mid-forceps procedures are avoided by the better attendants.[11] Babies were clearly meant to be pushed rather than pulled through the birth canal. Even at their more advanced stage of development, few adults would feel content to be pulled by the head out of a tight spot. And it is not just the baby who may fare poorly when forceps are used. Forceps may lacerate the vagina, extend an episiotomy to the rectum, and crack the tailbone. The use of forceps also usually requires anesthesia.

(5) Cesarean delivery has all the disadvantages of the major surgery

that it is. First there are the risks of an anesthesia accident, excessive bleeding, and damage to the urinary tract. If the surgery goes without incident, there is still a substantially increased risk of infection. This may result in a prolonged hospital stay and, in severe cases, may cause subsequent infertility. Even without infection, there is a long recovery. At a time of increasing responsibilities and major family adjustments, these problems can be particularly aggravating. The extended period of pain and incapacitation makes interaction with the new baby relatively difficult and introducing him to family (especially siblings) and friends stressful. In subsequent pregnancies the once-a-cesarean mother may be at risk for uterine rupture. Even in cases where that risk is exceedingly small, she may be regarded as an obstetrical cripple and therefore subject to interventions in labor that increase her chances of a repeat cesarean. Cesarean birth is not entirely benign for the baby either. The high incidence of respiratory distress syndrome, compared to vaginal birth, cannot be fully explained by the circumstances that lead to surgery.[12] It is possible in a cesarean section that the baby may inhale on exposure to the air before being removed from the uterus. If this happens, the baby may also breathe in amniotic fluid or blood. In contrast, passage through the vagina in a natural birth would tend to squeeze out any fluid that may be in the lungs before the first breath is taken.

Because these drawbacks are acceptable in those cases where vaginal birth is truly dangerous to the mother or child, they have come to be taken lightly in some quarters. In fact, although it runs directly counter to the recommendations of the recent National Institutes of Health Consensus Development Task Force on Cesarean Birth, some obstetricians still maintain that cesareans should be done even more frequently than they are, in order to insure consistently good babies. They argue that it is acceptable to do any number of unnecessary cesarean deliveries in order to catch the one baby who may benefit. This view fails to consider that, even if the outcome for the needy case is improved, the outcome for the other cases is certainly less satisfactory and the net effect beyond a certain point must be negative. The doctors who need to do many cesareans in order to deliver consistently good babies are those who

indulge most heavily in practices that increase the need for rescue oper-
ations. The general improvement in infant outcomes in recent years has
been found to have little to do with the parallel increase in cesarean
rates.[13]

Many doctors claim that they don't like doing medical deliveries, but
that our cultural attitudes toward birth, pain, and technology make it
necessary. If that's the case, they should tell you so. If I were your
doctor, I would tell you: "This birth is your job because no one can
bring your baby into the world better than you. Not only can you do it
yourself, but you and your baby will be better off if you do. We will be
there to reassure you, and we will be there to help in the event that
something goes wrong. We will also take over if you make us, but
please don't make us. If you will trust your body and not suppress its
messages with medication, we will not need to burden you with prophylaxis. Without these two things, the outcome for you and your baby will
be the best possible." Why doesn't your doctor tell you this? Either he
doesn't believe it, or he's afraid you won't believe it, or both. He may
think that, even without medication, prophylaxis is important or at least
does no harm. He may think that you will want, will need, or should
have pain medication. You may think so too. In the next few chapters
I'd like to convince you (and him, if he's reading this) that no medication / minimal prophylaxis is the best way to go, if at all possible. To
do this I will discuss each corner of the pain-relief / prophylaxis / med-
ical-delivery triangle.

4

LADIES IN DISTRESS

FIRST, let's talk about your side of the proposed bargain. You and your doctor may think that someone who has never given birth without pain medication can't possibly know what it means to agree to such a course. The fact is, however, that if you give careful consideration to your knowledge of pain from other situations, you will come to appreciate that pain is the most misunderstood and most unjustly maligned aspect of childbirth.

Pain is your body's signal to take heed. By its nature, it commands your prompt attention to the situation. The severest pain is that associated with surgery. It tells you that your body is being assaulted in the most extreme way. However, chances are that you already know this, accept it, and don't want to do anything about it. In this situation, the message that pain brings is useless, causes unnecessary distress, and is best suppressed by whatever means are available (including drugs, hypnosis, and acupuncture).

In general, however, the message that pain brings is very useful. The pain of a burn leads you to remove your body from the heat, preventing further damage. To relieve the pain, you submerge the burned skin in cool water, thereby drawing heat from the area. In a continuing effort to minimize the pain, you keep air from the skin with a salve, which controls dehydration, and avoid other contact with the area, which prevents infection and further trauma. In this case, pain leads you to deal constructively with an affront to your body. Similarly, the pain of hunger leads you to eat, and the pain of cold leads you to seek shelter. When you receive a blow, the pain leads you to apply pressure to the affected area; this minimizes blood loss from broken blood vessels. Similarly, the pain of a headache leads you to seek calm surroundings to relieve the tension that caused or exacerbated the problem.

To ignore pain in any of these situations is clearly foolhardy. Measures that reduce the pain are clearly in your best interest. Pain is your built-in manual for self-preservation and repair. If you throw it away, you're in trouble. This fact is well recognized in most areas of medicine. Even with the highly sophisticated diagnostic tools available today, pain is still an important indicator of illness, and the absence of pain is still an important sign of well-being. Indeed, there are specific medical procedures in which pain medication is withheld because the perception of the degree and nature of pain is the quickest and most reliable indicator of how things are going.

The question, then, is whether the pain in childbirth is the useless kind that obtains in surgery or the useful kind that obtains more generally. The answer depends upon what you're going to do about it. If the answer, as in surgery, is nothing, then you are caught in a dilemma. Medication will make your labor less effective, with a less-than-optimal outcome for you and your baby. In addition, it will be in your baby's system for hours or days after birth with known and unknown consequences, both long-term and short-term.[1] Without medication, the distress caused by the pain can lead to muscle tension. In addition to being exhausting, this aggravates the pain by fighting the contractions and increases the chances of fetal distress or failure to progress by reducing blood flow to the baby and the uterus.[2] The dilemma can be reduced somewhat by using hypnosis or distraction (e.g., breathing patterns and focal points), instead of medication, to suppress the pain. However, such conventional approaches to natural childbirth are not always effective and are not constructive responses to pain. The dilemma can be avoided entirely by accepting the pain as a useful message and seeking natural ways to relieve it. In so doing you will make your labor more effective and improve your baby's environment.

In fact, the physical consequences of natural measures to reduce pain in labor are strikingly good. For example, many women find that walking in the first stages of labor reduces pain. Indeed, women who have discovered this often refuse to sit or lie down, to the chagrin of attendants and fetal monitor suppliers.[3] As it happens, walking and movement generally also increase the effectiveness of labor. Similarly, many women find that they become nauseous or lightheaded if they lie on their backs during late pregnancy and childbirth. By resting instead on their sides, mothers avoid compressing the major blood vessels that carry blood to and from the uterus and the baby. A less common occurrence is that of back pain in labor. This typically occurs when the baby faces the mother's pubic bone (posterior presentation) instead of the tailbone (anterior presentation). Getting on all fours is often helpful in relieving this pain. It so happens that getting on all fours also can help the baby rotate to the normal, anterior presentation.[4] In the second stage of labor, many women find that squatting in some manner makes pushing more comfortable. The baby also descends more quickly in this position. With flexed legs and an upright position, the tension of the body's weight braced against firmly planted feet pulls the ischia apart. This traction, and the relaxation of the connective tissue induced naturally by relaxin, expands the pelvis.[5] An upright position also makes the best use of gravity and reduces the incidence of tearing by distributing the pressure on the vaginal outlet more evenly.

The most common cause of excessive pain in childbirth is tension. Relaxation reduces the pain by restoring the blood supply to the uterus and to the baby and by reducing muscular resistance to contractions. Again, the pain is a sensitive indicator of suboptimal conditions, and correction makes the labor more effective and improves the outcome for the baby. Relaxation exercises are included in childbirth classes for this reason. But, although there is no question that such techniques are useful for dealing with unavoidable stress (in fact, they can be used with good effect for minimizing pain in other circumstances), much of the tension in childbirth is unnecessary.

Tension may have a variety of origins. The most well recognized of these is fear.[6] Originally, the development of childbirth education was directed specifically at removing ignorance as a source of fear. However, even the best-informed person may approach childbirth anxiously if she anticipates that various people (most of whom she has never met before) will, with the best of intentions, feel free, or even obligated, to intrude and to give directives when she is in labor. No matter how self-confident, informed, or articulate you may ordinarily be, labor is not the time to have to defend your wishes for yourself or your baby. No matter how thoughtful and forgiving you generally are, labor is not the time to have to be considerate of anyone else's needs or routines. Too often, childbirth classes focus on what others will expect of you in the way of cooperation with various procedures and rules. It is vital for your comfort and the well-being of your baby that you make sure that those who will be involved in your care understand what you expect of them.

Aside from the unresolved concerns that you may bring to the situation, tension may be caused by environmental irritants. Active labor requires undivided attention. Even mild disturbances, such as changes in lighting and relocation from one place to another, cause labor abnormalities and increased stillbirth in animals. Although the effects of such disturbances on humans are mitigated by the ability of the mother to comprehend their purpose and the ability of attendants to rescue babies in distress surgically, it is clear that disturbances in labor should be minimized.

It is also vital that you feel in control of your environment. Unfortunately, the question of control is generally seen by both physicians and patients as purely a social or political issue. However, it is also most emphatically a medical issue. Environmental irritants cause less stress in an individual (as measured by various physiological indicators) if they are under the individual's control, *even* if she does not choose to exercise that control.[7] Thus you should be sure that you will be free to exercise all of the choices that you anticipate may be of even the slightest importance to you in labor. Legally, it is your right to exercise these choices. However, you and your chosen attendants need to be comfortable with that understanding. I think that one reason that pain is not a

FIGURE 7. GETTING COMFORTABLE

A. By lying on your side you can rest without compressing important blood vessels. While pushing in this position, it is helpful to have someone support your upper leg.

B. On all fours you can minimize pressure on your back while still working with gravity.

C. You can squat easily with support on each side.
D. A single assistant can also help you squat by supporting you from behind. He should lean a little from the knees (as shown) to avoid straining his back.

(Patricia Cobb)

central issue in home births is that control is also not a central issue in that setting. Environmental disturbances are minimized, and all activities are at the discretion of the mother. Homelike décor in an alternative birthing room cannot substitute for this aspect of homebirth.

Several authors[8] and many mothers have noted the similarities between childbirth and intercourse. These include unusual muscular strength, restricted sensory perception, rhythmic contractions of the uterus, breathing pattern and facial expression at culmination, and sudden return of awareness and emotional reaction of deep satisfaction at completion. Like intercourse, birth reaches fruition more readily if you feel secure enough to lose yourself in it. Like intercourse, birth is painful if you resist it and frustrating if you are self-conscious or if your partner is insensitive to your needs. If you are going to let cultural preconceptions (exemplified by such language as "confinement," "lying-in," and "birth pains"), social inhibitions, environmental constraints, attendants' expectations, and authoritarian expertise prevent you from doing your body's bidding, you will have a tougher labor and a more stressed baby than necessary. Childbirth is no more ladylike than conceiving was in the first place. The problem is that on this end you have less privacy and those around you are less personally involved. It is important, therefore, to pick an environment and cultivate a mindset such that you won't worry about what people will think if you pace, jiggle, or squat, moan, groan, or grunt, throw off clothes, spend the whole labor in the shower, or otherwise do what makes your labor more comfortable.

Child psychologists have long been concerned that a naïve observer might interpret behavior in intercourse as indicative of a painful struggle. So, too, the noises, facial expressions, postures, and motions that a mother might find useful in labor may be interpreted, even by many professionals, as begging for medication. Intense effort is easily misconstrued as pain. You should make sure, therefore, that the people you expect to look to for emotional support and guidance not be naïve about natural behavior in labor.

Most labors have a very consuming and difficult period toward the end of the first stage. The uterine muscles are working extremely hard at this point, and they feel like it. This great effort may also be associated with trembling and hot and cold sensations, with irritability, disorientation, and discouragement, and with extreme sensitivity to touch and suggestion. Since this period is usually short, medication given as a substitute for reassurance at this time usually takes effect when no longer needed. It also interferes with the progress of the second stage, lingers in the baby's body after birth, and deprives the mother of the boost to her confidence that she richly deserves to launch her into motherhood. A good labor assistant will tell you that intense and even disorienting sensations at the end of the first stage are a good sign of progress and that your baby's birth is getting close.

The importance of experienced support in labor cannot be overemphasized. All women who have given birth without pain medication insist that without the continuous encouragement and guidance of a good labor assistant they could not have done it. In some cases, the maternity-unit nurses offer effective guidance and support. But this is hit or miss. Some nurses are not well suited either by temperament or training to provide the kind of help that is needed in natural childbirth. In addition, the unit may be too busy or too understaffed for a nurse to stay with one woman throughout her active labor. In any case, as a complete stranger she may not be able to relate to the patient well enough to do a good job. In this respect the woman's husband (or another close friend) might do better, and natural childbirth classes try to prepare him for this role. However, most husbands cannot substitute for an experienced labor assistant who knows the many variations of labor, who recognizes the signs of each stage, who has a repertoire of helpful comments and suggestions, and whose experience enhances her credibility in the mother's eyes. For this reason, some obstetricians require that patients who have previously had cesarean deliveries have the help of an experienced labor assistant. (In these births, it is generally advised that pain medication be withheld to avoid masking faintness or any other signs of internal bleeding, that labor proceed as smoothly as possible to minimize stress on the uterus, and that strong positive reinforcement compensate for any psychological damage remaining from the previous

FIGURE 8. LABOR SUPPORT IN ANCIENT GREECE

Labor support has a long and honorable history. Here a squatting mother is supported by women on both sides and by a birth stool below, while two other women wait to receive the infant that is just appearing. *(From Speert[9])*

obstetric experience.) Increasing recognition of the great benefits of dedicated and experienced labor support has also motivated the organization of community-based groups of volunteer labor assistants in some hospitals.

The most striking demonstration of the value of labor support has come from a group of pediatricians.[10] Stimulated by the results of previous studies, they were interested in determining whether the presence of a supportive nonmedical woman during labor would influence postpartum mothering behavior. In order to reduce confounding variables, only mothers with uncomplicated labors (e.g., no oxytocin, analgesia, anesthesia, fetal distress, forceps, or cesareans) were observed after birth. Women were admitted randomly into the experimental group with labor support and the control group without labor support until there were 20 uncomplicated births in each group. One startling finding was that without labor support it took 103 women to get 20 uncomplicated cases, but with labor support it only took 33 women. When the uncomplicated cases were considered, further advantages to labor support became evident. The average length of time from admission to birth was 8.8 hours for the 20 mothers with support compared to 19.3 hours for the 20 mothers without support. Perhaps, as a consequence, the unsupported mothers were awake less than the supported mothers during the first hour after birth. However, even during their awake time the unsupported mothers showed significantly less affectionate behavior toward their infants than the supported mothers. In another study of similar design, complications arose in 61 percent of the control cases as compared to 34 percent of the experimental cases. Among those babies born with no problems, the number of common pediatric illnesses in the first six months of life was the same in both groups. However, the infants of mothers who had labor support were hospitalized significantly less often with these illnesses than the infants of mothers who were on their own.

Although physical support (e.g., in walking or squatting) is helpful in labor, the most important element of labor support is positive reinforcement. When long-distance runners are going the last mile, calls of

"Looking good," "You can do it," and "Go for it" help them do their best. Unfortunately, in our hospitals women in labor are more likely to hear "Are you sure you can manage?" "There's no need to suffer, you know," "If you think this is tough, just wait," and ultimately, when the natural process has slowed to a snail's pace, "Let's get this over with." Under these circumstances it is difficult for anyone, but most especially for a first-time mother, to maintain a positive attitude. An assistant who has confidence in natural childbirth and who, by virtue of her experience and personality, can convincingly project that confidence will help a mother stay on track in the "last mile."

With the help of an experienced labor assistant it is rare for a woman to need any pain medication (even in a difficult labor), unless surgery becomes necessary. But it is common, especially in first births, for women assisted only by husbands as bewildered and distressed as they are to lose their bearings and take pain medication. Although it is important that your mate be present for moral support and in his own right as an expectant parent, it is unfair to ask him to take responsibility for the conduct of the labor. If, however, it should become necessary for him to act as your assistant, it will help him to do a better job if he can keep in mind that your body is made to give birth and that it has a built-in mechanism, which we denigratingly call pain, to get you to cooperate and to enlist the support of others. If he concentrates on helping you find natural sources of comfort (a walk, a warm shower, vocalization, a leaning post, calm surroundings, control over irritants, relief of anxiety), he will be doing the best thing for you and your baby. If you are unfortunate enough to have a difficult labor, he should encourage you to accept it, to continue to seek natural sources of comfort, and to try to relax. But, if all else fails, he should let you scream. Genuine nontheatrical screaming is a good way to release tension. In fact, at least one obstetrician goes so far as to say that women who permit themselves to scream in labor do better than those who don't, because they are less inhibited and more accepting of their labor. In any case, screaming (in frustration rather than in terror) never hurt anyone, and it has the great advantage that it stops when the difficult phase of labor is over. Medication, on the other hand, takes a long time to wear off and can cause all sorts of trouble for both you and the baby in the mean time.

* * *

Pain, like other sensations, is a legitimate biological mechanism for coaxing you into behavior that nature considers to be in your best interests. The insistent quality of pain makes it particularly effective in situations, such as birth, that require your immediate attention. This effectiveness is defeated if the signals themselves are suppressed with medication, if your receptivity to the signals is suppressed by hypnosis or distraction, or if your responsiveness is suppressed through inhibitions and explicit or implicit prohibitions. A positive and responsive attitude toward pain in birth will improve the outcome for you and your baby, not only by avoiding the unnecessary use of drugs, but by generally improving the conduct of labor.

5

PRESCRIPTIONS FOR
DISASTER

RISK is an important concept in medicine in general and in obstetrics in particular. The term refers to the possibility of undesirable outcomes. Although there is no such thing as a risk-free pregnancy (or indeed a risk-free life), it is important to distinguish between different degrees of risk in order to make intelligent choices regarding prevention and treatment. In obstetrics, mothers and fetuses with characteristics that predispose them toward or are associated with an increased probability of undesirable outcomes are considered to be at high risk. Those with no such characteristics are referred to as low risk.

One important aspect of risk is its uncertainty. In spite of the increased probability of problems, many high-risk pregnancies conclude with no complications and no need for intervention. Nobody complains about this. However, when low-risk pregnancies become complicated and require rescue during labor, there is frequently shock and puzzlement. Because there are certain problems that cannot be anticipated in advance of labor, many obstetricians say that there is no such thing as a normal pregnancy until after the fact. However, others argue that conventional obstetrical practices add considerably to the complications that may occur in childbirth.

In the previous chapter, we discussed pain medication. Because pain medication has direct and indirect adverse effects on the labor and on the baby, a very strong argument can be made that its use automatically converts a low-risk pregnancy into a high-risk pregnancy. To be sure, some medicated labors, like other high-risk labors, conclude reasonably normally. There are even occasional cases (e.g., when there is intractable tension or an unusually premature urge to push) that are improved by light medication. However, in most cases, the probability that complications will arise and that intervention will be necessary is increased by medication. Before the popularization of prepared childbirth, anesthesia was used in virtually 100 percent of all hospital births in the United States. Although the rate has since decreased, anesthesia is still used in about 80 percent of the hospital births in the United States. Current obstetrical prophylaxis has developed in this context of a 100-percent to 80-percent artificially high-risk patient population.

The trade-off between costs and benefits is another important consideration in the development of medical protocols. A medical procedure is justified to the extent that it provides benefits exceeding its costs (in dollars and in social repercussions as well as in medical side effects). The benefit of obstetrical prophylaxis is in preventing problems that might otherwise occur. Obstetricians are proud to tell you that the benefit of fetal monitoring is in detecting fetal distress early enough to prevent permanent damage to the baby, that the benefit of *nihil per os* (literally, "nothing by mouth") is in preventing aspiration of vomited stomach contents under anesthesia, and that the benefit of an episiotomy is in substituting a straight, relatively easy-to-stitch cut for a tear. But what are the costs of these procedures, and how do they balance against the benefits? Clearly, the more probable and more formidable a problem is, the more desirable prevention becomes. For example, if you expect that left to your own devices you will probably sustain a big tear near the anus or the urethra and clitoris, you will want an episiotomy. On the other hand, if you consider it unlikely that you will sustain anything more than a small nick in the perineum, you will be most ungrateful for the cut, possible further tearing, multiple stitches, increased risk of infection, extended discomfort, and considerable scar tissue that comes with an episiotomy.[1]

The same argument can be made for fetal monitoring and *nihil per os*. It is not possible to discuss the desirability of these measures outside of the specific context in which they are to be used. In certain high-risk situations (including medicated birth), the benefits of these preventive measures probably exceed their costs. However, in low-risk births (by my definition, births free of medication as well as other significant risk factors), the benefits are lower and the costs are higher. Unfortunately, because they rarely have the opportunity to observe births unburdened by routine interventions, few obstetricians recognize the costs inherent in obstetrical prophylaxis and even fewer discuss them with their patients. The rest of this chapter is devoted to this important matter.

ELECTRONIC MONITORING

Electronic monitors provide a continuous record of the fetal heart rate and the tone of the uterus. The former provides a measure of the baby's well-being, and the latter tracks the timing and intensity of contractions. The fetal heart rate is measured most accurately by twisting a small spiral electrode into the baby's scalp, while uterine activity is most accurately measured by passing a pressure transducer past the baby's head into the uterine cavity. In addition to accuracy, this internal monitoring has the advantage of permitting the mother relatively free movement. With the wires protruding from the vagina taped to her thigh, in order to prevent their being yanked out of place, the mother can move about in bed or use a rocking chair. If a telemetry unit is available, the mother can carry it up and down the hall while it transmits information back to the recorder. However, because these units are expensive and don't work very well, they are few and far between. Internal monitoring has the great disadvantage of requiring the rupture of the amniotic sac, destroying the first defense against infection and the baby's fluid cushion. In addition, many parents remain unconvinced that the baby is oblivious to the electrode in his scalp.

External monitoring of the fetal heart rate is usually accomplished by strapping an ultrasound transducer around the mother's belly. Like the

Doptone (a brand of ultrasound stethescope) in the doctor's office, the external fetal monitor beams high-frequency sound waves at the baby which are reflected in a pattern (known as the Doppler shift) that provides a measure of heart activity. Uterine activity may also be monitored externally by strapping a second belt containing a tension gauge around the mother's abdomen. In order to provide useful information, the devices must be positioned carefully. Thus, in addition to coping with the annoyance of the straps themselves, the mother cannot rub her belly or move around. Extended exposure to ultrasound is also a matter of concern. Although no obvious damage has been associated with obstetric uses of ultrasound, subtle effects cannot be excluded. Ultrasound, with the duration and intensity used in extended monitoring, has been shown to cause changes in human cells.[2] The sad lesson from our experience with *DES* is that it can take a whole generation to discover the ill effects of certain agents.[3] The recent National Institutes of Health Consensus Development Task Force on the Diagnostic Uses of Ultrasound has called for greater discretion in the use of ultrasound until long-term safety studies are completed. External monitoring of the fetal heart rate can be accomplished without exposure to ultrasound by using electrocardiogram techniques. However, this is difficult, and the mother must stay still to avoid disturbing the electrical leads pasted on her belly.

Before electronic monitors were available, and even now when they are not used, the well-being of the baby during labor was followed by intermittent auscultation—that is, listening to his heartbeat periodically with a fetal stethoscope. Electronic monitors were greeted with enthusiasm because they supply more accurate and more detailed information than can be obtained by human auscultation.[4] In principle, this improved information would increase the likelihood of discovering a baby in trouble early enough to help him. Because the method did not involve drugs, and because ultrasound was assumed to be benign, no adverse side effects were anticipated and fetal monitoring was adopted nearly universally without testing.

Many mothers, babies, and dollars later, it appears that electronic monitoring rarely helps and sometimes hurts. Obstetricians have turned

FIGURE 9. EXTERNAL ELECTRONIC MONITORING

Typically, an electronic monitor is used with the mother lying on her back. This position increases the chances of fetal distress, inhibits labor, and increases pain (see Figures 2 and 6). *(Patricia Cobb)*

themselves inside out in an effort to demonstrate in properly designed studies that its routine use does help babies.[5] However, improved infant outcomes are only observed in the 7 to 8 percent of births that are at particularly high risk. These comprise cases with excess amniotic fluid (hydramnios), multiple pregnancy, placental or cord problems, malpresentation, or combinations of certain lesser risk factors. In other high-risk cases, such as pregnancy-induced hypertension, Rh disease, or diabetes, no advantage has been found.[6] In the general population, the improvement in the few cases with unsuspected problems is out-

FIGURE 10. AUSCULTATION

Auscultation allows the mother to be upright and ambulatory. This keeps pressure off the major blood vessels, reduces pain, and facilitates labor. *(Patricia Cobb)*

weighed by poorer outcomes in the great majority of cases. As one group of investigators wrote plaintively, this is "less dramatic than the results hoped for in the early days of this technology."[7]

Why is it that continuous electronic monitoring has proved so disappointing? There are only two possibilities. Either the information obtained is less useful than expected or it costs more than expected. The usefulness of the information depends very much upon the practitioner's skill in interpreting it. However, disappointing results are obtained even in hospitals with long-standing fetal monitoring programs and highly experienced practitioners. The cost of obtaining the information depends upon what the monitoring does to the mother and the baby. Superficially, it appears to do nothing, but in fact it does a great deal. It is well documented that ambulation improves the efficiency of labor, reducing both the duration and the pain. It is also well documented that, short of hanging by the feet, the supine position is the least effective and most dangerous position for labor. Internal electronic monitoring makes ambulation difficult, and external electronic monitoring discourages any movement from the supine position at all. When ominous tracings are seen on the monitor, the first step in fetal resuscitation is to roll the mother from her back to her left side. The irony is that, were it not for the monitor, the mother would probably not have been on her back in the first place.[8]

Monitoring also draws attention away from the labor. During active labor without a monitor, everyone in the room is focusing upon the physical demands of the moment. When an electronic monitor is in use, even the mother may be more attentive to the chart recorder than to body messages. By reducing the efficiency and comfort of the labor, monitoring an undrugged patient exacts a high cost in an increased need for pain relief and labor stimulants, with attendant consequences. On the other hand, if drugs are already in use, the balance between cost and benefit shifts in favor of monitoring. The benefit increases to the extent that the drugs or their side effects increase the chance of fetal distress. The costs decrease because the body messages that motivate beneficial behavior have already been suppressed and the mother is less able to respond anyway.

In the few specific high-risk situations in which fetal monitoring has been shown to improve infant outcomes, it is also associated with a decreased rate of cesarean delivery. In these special cases a good fetal monitor tracing provides attendants with the confidence to wait when they might otherwise have decided to intervene. In general, however, the use of fetal monitoring has been associated with increased cesarean rates, both as a historical trend and in comparison of contemporaneous groups.[9] Among some practitioners, excess cesareans may result from overdiagnosis of fetal distress. However, in hospitals with greater experience in electronic monitoring, the diagnosis of fetal distress has not increased. In these maternity units, the increase in cesarean rate in recent years is related to more frequent diagnoses of failure to progress, sometimes attributed to cephalopelvic disproportion (mismatch between the size of the baby's head and the mother's pelvis). The practitioners say these cesareans result from a greater disinclination to use forceps in recent years. However, this cannot explain the differences between contemporaneous groups. Until proven otherwise, it is more plausible that continuous fetal monitoring, by making labor less effective, is at least partially responsible for the increase in cesarean deliveries. The benefits of electronic accuracy and detail could perhaps better be realized by using the monitor like a stethoscope, by holding the sensor against the mother's abdomen for short periods of time. The main thing is to realize that it is not yet possible to detect every baby that is in trouble and that the cost of trying to do so is more troubled babies and more sectioned mothers. No protocol is risk-free, and it is the mother who should choose which risks are more acceptable to her.

NIHIL PER OS

The rationale for *nihil per os* (nothing by mouth, abbreviated NPO) is that stomach contents may be vomited and aspirated if anesthesia becomes necessary. Normally, gagging prevents liquid that gets into your throat from being sucked into your lungs when you breath. However, anesthesia suppresses the gag reflex. The severity of the lung damage (pulmonary aspiration syndrome) and the speed of recovery depend on both the composition (acidity and particulateness) and volume of the material aspired. In severe cases, it can compromise respiration to the extent of causing brain damage and death.

It is widely believed that gastric emptying (movement of food from the stomach into the small intestine, where it can no longer be vomited up) slows in labor. Anesthesiologists thus recommend that nothing further be taken by mouth once labor is suspected to have started. But consider a woman finishing dinner at 7 P.M., going to bed without a snack, and waking with contractions at 7 A.M. If she has an ordinary twelve-hour labor, she will have fasted about eighteen hours before the real work of active labor begins and twenty-four hours before her baby is born. To prevent dehydration and exhaustion, she may be given an IV. However, this is highly problematic. To begin with, the IV makes it physically and psychologically difficult to move around in the first stage and jockey for position in the second stage. It is an environmental irritant over which the patient ordinarily does not feel any control, with the consequences discussed in the previous chapter. In addition, without food, the fluid in the stomach becomes highly acidic, requiring periodic doses of antacid to reduce the threat to the lungs. This is frequently very repulsive to the mother. Furthermore, the wrong kind of antacid will actually aggravate pulmonary aspiration syndrome.[10]

The composition of an IV is also an inadequate substitute for water and food. The fluid must contain enough salt or sugar to keep the blood cells from swelling and popping as it goes in. The usual 5-percent dextrose (D-glucose) solution contains 21 Lifesavers' worth of sugar per 1-liter bag (about 1 quart of fluid). A 1-liter bag of the usual 0.9-percent saline or lactated Ringers (a buffered salt solution) contains as much sodium as an entire day's worth of the average American's diet but less than half as much water. Since the intake is not regulated by appetite, mother and baby can get too much sugar or salt. Excess salt is excreted slowly and will cause water retention, swollen tissues, and possibly even respiratory problems in the meantime.[11] Excess sugar is normally removed from the blood by the liver (which strings the molecules together for storage) in response to circulating insulin. When sugar is taken by mouth, the first signal for insulin production comes from the intestines *before* the sugar even reaches the blood. In addition, since the blood from the intestines is shunted directly to the liver, much of the sugar taken in is removed from the blood before reaching the general circulation. In contrast, when sugar is taken by vein, the initial stimulus to insulin production and the first pass through the liver are missing. Thus maternal blood sugar increases well above the normal range. Since sugar crosses the placenta freely, fetal blood sugar also rises above normal, in spite of the baby's production of his own insulin. In this induced diabetic state (hyperglycemia), the baby becomes prone to low blood pH (acidosis) and fetal distress.[12] Once born, however, and abruptly removed from the maternal supply of sugar, the baby's abnormally high insulin level causes his blood sugar to plummet to below normal. This condition (hypoglycemia) may greatly complicate his adjustment to extrauterine life. In addition, sugar IVs in labor are associated with an increased risk of neonatal (newborn) jaundice, requiring extended hospitalization for phototherapy.[13]

Other than a surfeit of sugar and salt, the standard IV solutions contain no nutrients that might be important for extended strenuous and stressful activity or a normal response to pain. Certainly, few people would want to climb a mountain or move a household with only a mixture of salt and sugar water in lieu of breakfast, lunch, and dinner. In fact, you might very well get sick to your stomach on this diet of liquid candy, as do many women laboring under these circumstances. Although women who overeat in labor may vomit, they usually feel better after they do. In contrast, the on-again, off-again dry heaves of a woman fed intravenously in labor are painful and do not alleviate the nausea. All things considered, it seems a foregone conclusion that a woman with a gentle, gradually progressing labor is likely to get stuck before the end, with or without an IV, if she does not eat or drink anything after the first contraction.

The belief that gastric emptying is slow in labor is based on observations of medicated mothers lying in bed. However, lying down is known to slow digestion, and, even more to the point, pain medication

57

has been shown to slow gastric emptying (as well as intestinal activity) in nonpregnant volunteers. A study of unmedicated mothers has shown that at least during the latent phase of labor the rate of gastric emptying is normal.[14] Thus readily digestible foods eaten during the latent phase will not stay in the stomach long if medication is not used. The best foods are low in fat, which retards gastric emptying, and low in particulate residue (e.g., seeds or fibers), which is particularly difficult for the lungs to handle. Good foods include plain crackers, fruit purées, gelatin, and low-fat yoghurt.

During active labor, hunger is relatively rare, but thirst is common. Clear liquids (clarified broth and filtered juices) can satisfy the thirst and soothe the stomach (by reducing stomach acidity) while providing nourishment. Although there are no studies of gastric emptying during active labor, it is unlikely that clear liquids consumed in moderation will accumulate in the stomach. Water, the main constituent of these fluids, runs right through the body to the bladder in minutes. (That's why you are asked to drink water in the radiology department before a pelvic ultrasound.) Considering the biology involved, it is difficult to imagine a mechanism by which, or a rationale for which, the body would stem this movement in labor. Thus, by choosing foods judiciously and consuming them according to appetite, it should be possible in an unmedicated birth to satisfy the nutritional needs of labor without increasing the risk of pulmonary aspiration syndrome. In fact, the risk of pulmonary aspiration syndrome might even be decreased to the extent that the labor progresses better and there is less likelihood of an emergency requiring general anesthesia.

* * *

The prophylaxis used in modern obstetrics is motivated to a large extent by the hazards of medicated birth. In general, protocols developed for medicated birth are counterproductive for unmedicated birth because they ignore and frustrate natural feedback mechanisms. At the very least they sap your psychic and physical energy. Often, pain medication becomes necessary and medical delivery follows. Thus, the distrust of natural childbirth mechanisms inherent in heavy-handed prophylaxis is in large measure self-fulfilling. Unless your circumstances include one of the few specific risk factors or combinations of risk factors for which prophylaxis has had a demonstrated benefit, it is unwise to burden yourself with constraints that make nature's proven system less effective.

6

A MATTER OF TIME

MEDICAL delivery completes the triangle of controversial obstetrical practices that includes pain medication and prophylaxis. Medical delivery may involve the rupture of membranes, the administration of labor stimulants, episiotomy, instrumental delivery (using forceps or a suction cap), or cesarean delivery.

As a rule, you should expect an attendant to avoid medical delivery unless there is good reason to believe that intervention will improve the overall outcome for mother and child. Some cases are straightforward. If there are signs that the placenta is becoming detached prematurely *(abruptio placentae)* or that the placenta overlies the cervix *(placentae previa),* then a cesarean delivery is necessary to save the child's life. If tests show that the placenta is becoming functionally impaired, the child may be better off *ex utero* than *in utero* and labor may be induced. If a baby is transverse (lying crosswise in the uterus) or twins are locked, passage through the cervix is impossible and cesarean delivery is necessary.

Other cases are less clear-cut. Because traditional childbirth management (mother drugged, on her back, feet in the air) led to poor infant outcomes in vaginal breech deliveries (in which the baby exits butt or feet first instead of head first) and because cesarean delivery is less dangerous than it used to be, it has become customary in this country to deliver breech babies by cesarean. However, under favorable circumstances, and with an attendant experienced and confident in vaginal breech birth, cesarean delivery offers no recognized advantages.[1] It is also possible to maneuver breech babies into a normal presentation before labor starts. This procedure, known as external version, is coming back into use because, with drugs to relax the uterus temporarily and ultrasound to check for cord entanglement, its safety and success have greatly improved.[2]

In the United States, it has also been customary to do cesarean deliveries when the uterus has a scar from previous surgery. The rationale is that weak scar tissue may be strained to the breaking point during labor, if it hasn't already given way during the last weeks of pregnancy. Even an unscarred uterus can rupture during labor due to weakening by frequent pregnancy, multiple fetuses, excessive amniotic fluid, or overstimulation with oxytocin. In these cases, the rupture usually occurs in the fundus, and a fresh tear in this region produces very heavy bleeding. As a result, the baby often dies, and a hysterectomy is often necessary to control hemorrhage. However, such catastrophic situations are rare in scar separation, especially if the previous surgery involved only the lower segment of the uterus, as is now customary.[3] For these reasons, and because cesarean delivery is not as safe for mother or child as vaginal delivery, the "once a cesarean, always a cesarean" dictum was never adopted in Europe. The National Institutes of Health Consensus Development Task Force on Cesarean Birth has recently recommended that cesareans should no longer be repeated automatically in this country.

When there is concern about scar separation, the most constructive strategy is to minimize the amount of work that the uterus needs to do. To this end, it is important to use gravity to full advantage and to relax as thoroughly as possible. The benefits of gravity are maximized by walking as much as possible during the active part of the first stage, by squatting (which also increases the size of the pelvic outlet) or assuming some other vertical position during the second stage, and by eating according to appetite to maintain the strength to do these things. Relaxation may be facilitated by walking to minimize discomfort, by taking hot showers and sucking ice chips as desired, by excluding unnecessary strangers, by including family and other support people of choice, and by arranging a clear understanding in advance with all parties of what is expected under various circumstances.

The most questionable medical deliveries are those in which time is the main issue. Doctors frequently induce labor within a few weeks of the presumed due date, even when there are no signs that the baby's lifeline is compromised,[4] and within a few hours of rupture of membranes, even when there are no signs of infection. They commonly augment contractions (by rupturing membranes and/or using drugs) in the latent phase, even though no adverse effects are associated with a long latent phase if the mother is properly nourished. They often use forceps and / or an episiotomy to shorten the second stage, even without evidence of fetal distress. In addition, the most prevalent and most rapidly increasing indication for cesarean delivery has been failure-to-progress or cephalopelvic disproportion (CPD). In practice these diagnoses usually mean only that cervical dilation or fetal descent was not fast enough by some criterion. Indeed, the report of the National Institutes of Health Consensus Task Force on Cesarean Childbirth states that "there is compelling reason to examine the diagnostic category of dystocia (i.e., dysfunctional labor) because of its prominent association with the increase in primary cesarean birth rate and the absence of a survival advantage for the cesarean births over 2500 grams (i.e., over 5 lbs 8 ozs)." In other words, cesareans done to end slow labors form a large and particularly suspect group. In fact, with the demise of the "once a cesarean always a cesarean" doctrine, we are seeing women who were once sectioned for CPD giving birth to *larger* babies vaginally.

Considering the many factors that influence labor, it should not be surprising that time often becomes an issue. To begin with, as discussed in Chapter 2, anxiety has a potent inhibiting effect on labor. Women may worry that the baby will be born at an inconvenient time: while their husband is away on business, before getting settled in a new home, before the holidays are over, before Grandma comes to take care of the older children, or before a big project at work or at home is completed. As a result the baby considerately waits until the coast is clear. (Indeed, it is striking that some women, especially working women, have their babies only on Sundays.) It is also well known that women who are anxious about home birth need to go to a hospital in order to labor well. On the other hand, it is commonplace for a labor that has been good and steady at home to stop as soon as the mother enters the hospital or if the father leaves for one reason or another. (Although it is more unusual, I even know of a woman whose labor would stop in mid-contraction every time the doctor entered the room and resume when he left.) In these cases the mother's body is generating biochemical messages that act to suppress labor. The most sensible response, as we saw earlier in the case of pain, is to try to address the cause of the messages. Overriding them with medical intervention introduces unnecessary stress, as well as a risk of prematurity due to uncertainties in due dates. The FDA has outlawed the use of drugs for the elective induction of labor—that is, induction for the sake of convenience. However, the distinction between elective and nonelective induction is not always a clear one.

The issue of time becomes more serious when the membranes have ruptured spontaneously or have been ruptured surgically (in an effort to induce or strengthen labor or in association with the placement of internal electronic monitoring devices). Ordinarily, the membranes protect against infection by keeping bacteria out and amniotic fluid in. Since amniotic fluid is usually bacteriostatic (inhibiting of bacterial growth), bacteria that do penetrate normally cannot create a full-blown infection. But once the membranes are broken, a race between birth and infection begins. Fortunately, if the mother is well hydrated, some amniotic fluid is produced continuously which, in addition to lubricating the uterine and vaginal walls, helps to flush bacteria away. Although bacteria can move against this flow to infect the uterus, the incidence of infection is more strongly related to the number of vaginal exams done after the membranes rupture than with the actual time elapsed. This may seem odd, in that doctors routinely take care to introduce only sterile objects (whether gloved fingers or fetal monitor sensors) into the vagina. However, no matter how sterile an object may be at the outset, by the time it reaches the uterus it is covered with mucus from the lower end of the vagina. This mucus contains bacteria that have no business in or near the uterus.

When the membranes rupture, it is important to make sure that the umbilical cord has not and cannot slip ahead of the baby and be pinched. (If the cord is prolapsed, it must be pushed back or the baby must be delivered abdominally. But if the baby's head is firmly down on the cervix so that there is no danger of cord prolapse, it is safe to walk around to stimulate contractions and increase comfort.) From this point on, vaginal examinations should be scrupulously avoided until it is clear that the birth is imminent—that is, until the mother feels the urge to push or labor has been active long enough to expect that dilation is well advanced. In fact, vaginal examinations should be minimized in early labor even if the membranes are intact because examinations may be disturbing and there is always some risk that the examination itself will cause the membranes to rupture. As a rule, an examination should only be done when the information gained will affect a choice that needs to be made in the conduct of the labor.

The passage of time also becomes critical when the mother is forbidden to eat or drink. If her labor starts before breakfast and the latent phase is long, the baby may be born twenty-four hours after her last meal. In such cases an IV will be necessary to prevent dehydration and provide some sugar. If that isn't enough to keep her going and oxytocin does not succeed in rousing the uterus to a last-ditch effort, an instrumental or cesarean delivery may be necessary. If dilation is complete and the baby is partially descended, forceps or a vacuum cap may be used to pull the baby out. If the baby has not descended enough, failure to progress or CPD will be diagnosed and a cesarean delivery performed.

Medical delivery, in one form or another, is often required when anesthesia is used. Indeed, it is so commonplace to have to stimulate contractions with oxytocin when epidural anesthesia is given (as well as vice versa) that the effects of the two drugs on newborns have been difficult to separate in scientific studies.[5] In contrast, arrested labors are relatively uncommon in unmedicated, well-nourished mothers. Preliminary data indicate that ambulation is as effective as oxytocin for reviving an arrested labor.[6] But this alternative may not be safe for those using analgesia and is not possible for those using anesthesia. Forceps (or vacuum extraction) are also relied upon heavily in medicated deliveries.[7] In contrast, in an unmedicated delivery the mother will, in the words of one doctor, "push the baby out if it comes down, or have a cesarean delivery if it does not." Instrumental delivery has virtually no place in unmedicated births. Indeed, forceps would probably not have been invented if cesarean delivery had been a safe alternative at the time.

Time may become an issue even when the membranes are intact and the mother is not medicated or fasting. As discussed in Chapter 2, the duration of labor is highly variable. However, only certain specific patterns of labor outside the wide range of normal ones are associated with poor outcomes. For example, an abnormally long latent phase is not associated with any special problems and does not call for any intervention. When abnormally protracted patterns of labor are associated with problems, it has generally been assumed that the passage of time per se is the cause of the problem and that forcing normal progress by using oxytocin or forceps will improve matters. This very loose logic has caused a great deal of damage. It is now known that the relatively poor outcomes associated with prolonged second stages are entirely due to the greater use of forceps to hurry things along.[8] In the absence of such intervention, slow second stages with normal monitoring produce normal results. The use of episiotomy to shorten the second stage is also not justified unless there are signs of fetal distress. One midwife relates that, when she was required to do sixteen mediolateral episiotomies during her training, she swore that she would never do another unless the baby was in trouble. In six years of active practice since then she has not had to do a single one.

Unfortunately, the notion that labor should adhere to a brisk schedule seems to have taken on a life of its own. When queried about the use of oxytocin, a serious young specialist on fetal distress recently told medical students that "women now expect to have their babies within 12 hours of admission to the hospital, so *you have to do something*" (emphasis added). This rationale is medically indefensible, but it is also sociological nonsense. If women expect to have their babies within twelve hours of entering the hospital, it is because doctors have taught them to expect that and because hospital protocols and routines make it difficult to carry on any longer than that. If doctors think that their patients are laboring under false expectations, so to speak, then it is their obligation to educate them accordingly.

There is no question that the judicious use of oxytocin can occasionally obviate a cesarean delivery and that cesarean delivery is occasionally necessary for a truly contracted pelvis (such as may result from childhood malnutrition or disease).[9] However, most medical deliveries can be avoided by attending to the mother's emotional state, minimizing prophylaxis and drugs, and encouraging the mother to cooperate with the labor (e.g., by walking in the first stage and squatting in the second stage). Even when doctors recognize the importance of these factors, they often wait until the labor is on the verge of failing before taking the appropriate measures. For example, thinking that a woman's labor is being inhibited by what is going on around her, the doctor may arrange for her to be transferred to a private labor room. In another case, a doctor who routinely uses fetal monitoring may abandon it when he sees how much difficulty it is causing his patient. In a third case, the doctor may allow the mother to eat when she is getting exhausted near the end of the birth, even though food is more dangerous when the labor is on the verge of failing than at any other time. In a fourth case, the doctor may permit the mother to squat for the second stage if she thinks of it, even though he never suggests it to a patient who is having trouble getting her baby down. Although these doctors are more sensitive than many of their colleagues, they are not taking the initiative early enough or often enough. Too frequently, they wait until some harm, if only exhaustion and discouragement, has already been done. In other practices, the harm is never even noticed. Too often, the physician's motto of *primum non nocere* ("above all, do no harm") has in practice meant that it is acceptable to do anything that is not clearly harmful. It would be more appropriate to shift the burden of proof in obstetrics so that protocols are limited to those that are clearly beneficial.

*   *   *

In current obstetrical practice, the various forms of medical delivery are used most often to force labor to progress according to a prescribed schedule. However, in unmedicated birth, the passage of time itself is rarely a source of trouble, and the outcomes of slow labors are rarely improved by intervention. Natural measures to promote the strength and effectiveness of labor—nourishment and rest, privacy and encouragement, ambulation and squatting—are far safer. At the same time, occasional monitoring should reassure all parties of the infant's well-being. A healthy outcome is all that matters. If your labor is slow, it may be because your body and your baby work best at that pace. Give them a chance. The medical options will still be there if you truly need them in the end.

II

Negotiating Supportive Obstetrical Care

7

A PERSONAL PROTOCOL

ASSUMING that you now have a good idea what kind of care you want and why, the rest of this book is devoted to helping you get it. One of the decisions you will be making is whether to separate your primary care from your medical backup. At this time, most women still place the responsibility for all of their maternity care with an obstetrician in a hospital. This therefore is the main context of this book. However, obstetricians and hospitals are only necessary for medical backup in the event of complications, and you may be able to put together a better package by making other arrangements for primary care (see Chapter 8). With some adaption, the process described here should help you decide whether an alternative arrangement will work best for you.

The foundation for successfully negotiating appropriate obstetrical care is a *written* list of preferences. This statement of the protocol that you wish observed in childbirth has several important purposes. To begin with, preparing it will help you to clarify your thoughts. If your ideas are vague, it will be difficult for you to carry them through. Once you have chosen an obstetrician, the list will also provide a reference point for discussing his style of care, defining areas of agreement, and resolving areas of disagreement (see Chapter 10). In fact, some progressive physicians request such a list to avoid misunderstandings and to protect themselves if the requests are unconventional (see Chapter 8). The list will also be a useful vehicle for introducing yourself and your preferences to the nursing staff of the hospital and enlisting their cooperation with your plans (see Chapter 9). Finally, the list will make it easier for your mate and your labor assistant to help you get the kind of obstetrical care that you want. Neither of these people can make decisions on your behalf. This is between you and the medical staff. But your husband and your labor assistant can remind the staff of the preferences that you have expressed, and this will be easier if the preferences are in writing, with copies distributed to all concerned.

In preparing your list, you should focus on the intrapartum and early postpartum periods. This is when the pressure of time and the physical and psychological demands of the moment make it difficult to make, express, and enforce choices. To organize your thoughts and make your intent as clear as possible, it is helpful to divide your list into sections for normal conditions and complications, and subdivide these chronologically according to the various stages of childbirth. The sample list at the end of this chapter illustrates this form of organization.[1] It is prefaced by identifying information and a short general statement of purpose and philosophy. The statement should provide a context for the specific items that follow. Different women may make the same requests for different reasons. As clearly and as succinctly as possible, you should explain the overall motivation for your requests and the spirit in which they are intended. This should allow care providers to see the connections between specific requests that can help them to provide consistently supportive care.

In outlining your requests, you should consider as many different scenarios as possible. Imagine various situations, and think about what you would want from the people around you under those circumstances and how you would hope the scene would play itself out. Even in normal circumstances this may not be as easy as it seems. It may not occur to you that some hospitals do not allow women to walk from the lobby to L&D (i.e., the labor and delivery unit) or that it may be uncomfortable to ride in a wheelchair or on a stretcher while in active labor. It also may not occur to you that even if you have no medication, some doctors and nurses will feel compelled to tell you when and how to push (often sooner and usually harder than your body tells you). You also may not expect that, even under normal circumstances, L&D staff may consider their neonatal procedures (examination, eye treatment, washing, weighing, etc.) to have more urgency and priority than yours (holding, nursing, interacting, etc.). Because such things are legitimately difficult to anticipate, it is important to learn as much as you can about the routines followed in your area. A good way is to talk to new mothers about the details of their birth experiences. In addition, tours of local maternity units provide opportunities to ask the staff about their standard operating procedures (see Chapter 9). As you learn from these encounters, you will probably want to amend your protocol. You should therefore expect to prepare several drafts before reviewing it with your doctor and sending it to the hospital.

As we have seen, many childbirth issues have to do with time. People often worry about getting to the hospital in time for a very short labor, but few give careful thought to the greater likelihood of a long labor. You should allow for the chance that one or more stages of labor may be long. Providing for rest and nourishment to prevent exhaustion, and physical and social activity to prevent boredom and frustration will be important if you have a long latent phase. The use of Pitocin will also be an issue under these circumstances, particularly if the membranes have ruptured. If active labor is prolonged, constructive responses to pain assume paramount importance. These require freedom to move around, reassurance, and continued nourishment. If contractions are strong and frequent, Pitocin will no longer be suggested. However, if progress is slow, cesarean delivery is likely to be discussed. In the second stage of labor, progress can be facilitated by assuming an upright posture with legs flexed. (This position also effectively denies access for forceps and episiotomy—see Chapter 12.)

The boundary between normal circumstances and complications may be difficult to define. Some obstetricians would consider a forceps delivery under anesthesia to be uncomplicated. The sample list of childbirth requests given here categorizes any situation warranting operative delivery (instrumental or surgical) as complicated. In the event of complications, your protocol should be aimed at minimizing physical and psychological trauma. Physical concerns include the accurate diagnosis of fetal distress, the use of antacids, the timing of cesarean delivery, the choice of forceps delivery, and the avoidance of the supine position.[2] Psychological concerns have to do more generally with questions of dignity and the importance of claiming the birth and the baby.

Your personal protocol should end with a list of the individuals who will receive copies. These are the people who, according to the hierarchy of the particular hospital, will be responsible for the care you and your baby receive. Although you can circulate blind copies to others, the written list of recipients says in effect that you ask these particular individuals to give serious attention to your preferences and to be aware that their colleagues are asked to do likewise. In addition, the protocol should be stapled to any authorization form that you are asked to sign in registering or preregistering at the hospital. Above your signature add a notation indicating that consent is given "in accordance with the attached letter." This will help ensure that your requests are taken seriously.

A PERSONAL PROTOCOL

CHILDBIRTH REQUESTS

TO:	The Best Hospital
PARENTS:	You and Your Mate
ESTIMATED DUE DATE:	
OBSTETRICIAN:	(including backup)
LABOR ASSISTANT:	(including backup)
PEDIATRICIAN:	
SIBLING(S):	Baby's Sister(s), Baby's Brother(s)
COMPANION FOR SIBLING(S):	(including backup)

I have chosen to give birth at The Best Hospital because I would like to have the benefits of medical assistance at hand, should it be needed. However, I believe that the need for such assistance is infrequent when physical and psychological encumbrances are minimized and physical and psychological support are maximized. I therefore request that, other than intermittent auscultation of the fetal heart and occasional measurement of my vital signs, the activities of those in my room be limited to providing personal encouragement and nonmedical assistance, unless

(a) signs of emergency dictate rapid intervention, or

(b) a leisurely and informed discussion has taken place of the benefits and risks of a proposed procedure, maneuver, or examination and, after some time for private consideration, my agreement has been ascertained.

It should be understood that I consider disconcerting pain lasting for more than a few contractions to be an indication of physical or psychological problems (e.g., malposition or anxiety). If I complain of pain, I would like help with the problem rather than the symptom. Medication for pain should be a last resort, considered only if *all* alternative approaches to pain relief have failed.

Other requests are listed below. I trust that they will be taken seriously as each one was included after a great deal of thought. If there are any impediments to honoring these requests, please inform me as soon as possible so that I may make other arrangements.

Normal Circumstances:

Option of walking from admitting to L&D

Use of birthing room and own clothes

Mate, labor assistant, and siblings present at my discretion at all times.

Use of shower, as desired

Light foods (i.e., with no fat or particulate residue), as desired (in moderation), during the latent phase of labor

Ice chips and clear liquids, as desired (in moderation), during active labor

No routine prep (shaving), enema, antacids, or confinement to bed

Absolute minimum of time attached to things (IV, monitor)

Try to use external ECG, if continuous monitoring necessary (to minimize exposure to ultrasound)

No stripping or artificial rupture of membranes, without prior discussion of alternatives and consequences, and some private time for consideration

As few examinations as possible (especially if membranes rupture early) and explanation beforehand of the need for the information to be obtained

Examinations as gentle as possible (to protect membranes and uterine scar*)

No labor stimulants of any kind, without prior discussion of alternatives and consequences, and some private time for consideration

No pain medication of any kind, without prior discussion of alternatives and consequences, and some private time for consideration

Choice of position in second stage (in or out of bed, including squatting, standing, kneeling, and use of portable commode or my own birthing stool)

No coaxing or exhortation (e.g., to push)

Choice of position for birth (in or out of bed, including squatting, standing, kneeling, and use of portable commode or my own birthing stool)

No episiotomy, unless the baby's condition requires expedited delivery

Cord cut only after it has stopped pulsing

No traction on the cord or administration of oxytocin to deliver the placenta

---

*When there has been prior uterine surgery (e.g., a previous cesarean delivery)

A PERSONAL PROTOCOL

No palpation of uterine scar* without discussion of the indications (versus risk of infection)

Placenta not disposed of until we have had a chance to look at it†

No routine suctioning of the baby

All feeding done by mother, starting as soon as possible, and on demand thereafter

Postponement of neonatal procedures as long as possible

Neonatal procedures done in presence of one or both parents, with explanations of purposes and results

Vernix left on unless or until we ask to remove it

Discharge as soon as possible

Complications:

All previous requests honored to extent possible

Explanations given and explicit consent obtained for each procedure, except in an emergency

IV on mobile stand and in mid-forearm (so hand and wrist free for use)

Fetal scalp stimulation test and fetal blood pH measurement to verify suspected fetal distress

No high or mid-forceps

Low forceps only if suction cap not available and baby's condition requires rapid delivery

No analgesia or anesthesia for palpation of uterine scar*

No particulate antacids under any circumstances (a soluble antacid such as citrate may be taken before anesthesia if stomach is empty)

Allow labor to progress as far as is safe before surgery (so that the retraction ring will be as high as possible, the lower segment will be as thin as possible, and the baby will have as nearly normal stimulation as possible)

† For those who are interested

Regional anesthesia for surgery, if possible, with no preoperative sedation

Left lateral tilt position for surgery or shift to supine position at the last possible moment

Arms / hands free at all times, when conscious

Mirror available to watch birth, if sterile field is blocked from my direct view†

Father present anytime he wants to be (especially if I am not conscious)

Shaving only as necessary

Incision at site of existing scar, if possible

Baby to stay in the recovery room with mother unless his / her condition requires immediate special attention elsewhere, in which case father will accompany him / her

Help with nursing and handling the baby in the recovery room

Ambulation and normal diet as soon as possible

COPIES TO: Chief of Obstetrics and Gynecology
Chief of Obstetrical Anesthesia
Chief of Neonatology
Director of Nursing
Director of Administration
Obstetrician (and backup)
Labor Assistant (and backup)
Pediatrician
Mate

8

THE BEST INTERESTS
OF ALL CONCERNED

ONCE you have developed a solid sense of the kind of care you want, you are ready to look for practitioners who will provide that care. However, in order to make sense of what you find, you need to have some appreciation of how things look from the other side.

Most of us expect that we need only find a caring and well-informed doctor, and that either we will convince him that what we want is as good as or better than the standard practice or he will convince us to the contrary. With the exception of an occasional charlatan, we are taught to expect that an obstetrician will do what is in our best interests as well as he understands them at that time. However, that expectation turns out to be naïve. Unfortunately, the merits of various obstetrical protocols tend to be overshadowed by the politics of obstetrics.

Looming large in this arena are the courts. Whether rightly or wrongly, doctors consider that in the event of a bad outcome the best defense against a suit is adherence to standard practice. It doesn't matter if recent research has shown that another way might be better. Bad outcomes occur occasionally under even the best care, and many doctors fear that the courts will not be able to judge that the care given was less likely to produce bad results than the standard practice. Most cases are settled out of court. In essence, the doctor's insurance company pays the plaintiff to drop any charges that might hold up in court. But the doctor's reputation is always on the line. It is this sense of vulnerability that causes the cesarean rate to rise in units that have recently had a perinatal death.

The legal knot is not easily loosened. On the one hand, it is difficult to find fault with doctors who seek to protect themselves from suit. At the same time, it is difficult to find fault with parents who seek compensation to ease the burden of a negligently hurt child. The key is in distinguishing negligence from the unavoidable limitations of even the best medical care. In this regard, obstetricians blame the public for unreasonable expectations. However, the profession has at times cultivated the impression of infallability and has generally failed to educate consumers meaningfully as to the limitations and potential adverse effects of its interventions. This failure of communication is aggravated by the development of large multiphysician practices which prevent women from forming sound relationships with their obstetricians.

The pressure on obstetricians to adhere to standard practice also takes more direct forms. Physicians depend for their livelihood upon their hospital privileges, licenses, and referrals. Some progressive practitioners have had their ability to practice destroyed by hostile colleagues who felt threatened by the responsive services that the progressive physicians were offering patients. Even their more open-minded colleagues may have subtle reservations. The doctor who sticks his neck out in such an antagonistic environment may be suspected of "ulterior motives," of not being good enough to attract patients except by providing unconventional services. While doctors on the progressive end of obstetrics work under great pressure from their colleagues, physicians at the other extreme practice outdated (sometimes euphemistically called "traditional") obstetrics with impunity. Older physicians generally do not feel comfortable disciplining a colleague for practices to which they themselves recently subscribed, and younger ones do not generally have the power to do anything about it.

Obstetricians also need to avoid alienating members of the hospital staff. Critical among these are the anesthesiologists. Obstetricians depend upon the good will of the anesthesiologists for patients who want anesthesia for vaginal deliveries or need it for cesarean deliveries. Some anesthesiologists become apoplectic when a woman eats or drinks during labor. (See Chapter 5.) Most obstetricians thus try to persuade women that eating in labor is not important. Failing that, they say they will agree to eating in labor if the anesthesiologist agrees, knowing full well he usually won't. More supportive doctors ask patients to stay near their own kitchens as long as possible and keep their intentions to eat to themselves until the time comes (counting on the anesthesiologist to behave himself when he finds out). Anesthesiologists may also take offense if a physician encourages a patient to do without anesthesia or to allow anesthesia to wear off for the second stage. Like anyone else, anesthesiologists like to feel needed. Unfortunately, some are not satisfied with being needed only for surgery.

Anesthesiologists are not the doctor's only concern on the hospital staff. A nurse may be uncooperative and may even complain (or threaten to complain) to officials if she disapproves of an obstetrician's departures from standard practice. To protect himself, the obstetrician who is supportive and indifferent to convention when the "right" nurse is in the room, may go by the book if the "wrong" one is assigned. The other side of the coin, of course, is that supportive nurses often feel very limited in what they can do for or how they can advise a patient without angering the attending physician and jeopardizing their jobs. Both groups feel safest sticking to the standard practice, whether they are convinced that it is best in a given case or not.

Because obstetricians are generally paid more for performing a cesarean delivery than for attending a vaginal birth, it is often assumed that money motivates some unnecessary cesarean deliveries. However, in an active practice, the fee is a minor consideration compared to time. In general, saving the doctor's time is by far the greater incentive for surgical delivery, as well as for the use of oxytocic drugs, episiotomy, and forceps. A large fraction of cesarean deliveries are for "failure to progress," often attributed to a pelvis too small to allow passage of the baby's head. However, maternity unit staff are well aware how rare true cephalopelvic disproportion is. Except for these occasional cases and a few unusual, less well-understood conditions, the diagnosis of cephalo-pelvic disproportion or failure to progress simply means that the doctor gave up before the baby was born (or that the mother's body was too frustrated to continue). It is becoming increasingly common for women who have had a section for cephalopelvic disproportion to disprove the diagnosis by subsequently delivering a larger baby vaginally. In our society, most of us feel under pressure of time, and an obstetrician is no different. He needs to arrange his activities very carefully to mini-mize the impact of this pressure on his practices. (This will be discussed in greater detail in Chapter 10.)

Physicians are not the only people you'll deal with whose interests may differ from yours. In particular, childbirth instructors need to be very careful about their conduct. Hospital instructors are in an espe-cially awkward position. They cannot openly criticize the practices employed by any member of the hospital staff without risking their jobs. As a result, discussion of the pros and cons of childbirth technology in hospital classes is often so wishy-washy as to be indecipherable. Inde-pendent community childbirth classes tend to be better, although many emphasize their own particular gimmicks for coping with contractions to the point of glossing over substantive issues and alternatives in the medical aspects of labor management. The best childbirth classes are usually those designed for couples planning home births. These classes emphasize personal responsibility, constructive attitudes, practical approaches, and common sense. This is the best preparation for birth in any setting. (Such classes and the contacts made there also help you to keep your options open regarding birth setting, should you eventually decide that the hospitals available to you are unacceptable.)

Unless they outnumber the physicians in their setting, midwives also function under severe political constraints. Traditionally the province of the midwife, supportive obstetrical care is now, in this country, most successfully and consistently offered in the home and in free-standing birth centers by women trained in these settings. However, in many areas, independent midwives have difficulty arranging for obstetrical backup. Midwives employed by hospitals have built-in backup. But the hospital incarnation of the midwife often lacks the training and the autonomy to practice truly supportive, noninterventionist care.

Institutions, like individuals, have interests to protect. In hospitals, an overriding concern is not to disturb the routine. That routine is organized to serve the general needs of attending physicians and their patients efficiently. But efficiency does not readily accommodate patients with individual preferences or labors that take their own time. This requires special attentiveness and flexibility, perhaps more than a busy staff can muster. A hospital also needs to keep its staff happy. Low staff morale and high staff turnover are bad for any operation. To avoid discontent, innovation can only be introduced when the staff is receptive. When conflict with an outsider occurs, the staff member will ordinarily receive the benefit of the doubt. Hospitals have banned private labor assistants who overstepped the boundary between assisting and nursing, as understood by the hospital staff.

In addition to the permanent staff, teaching hospitals must consider the needs of their trainees. These individuals work insane schedules at great cost to their personal lives in order to have the opportunity to learn and practice the skills of their profession. It is the obligation of the maternity unit to provide those opportunities to residents in obstetrics and gynecology and in obstetrical anesthesiology. In practice, each hospital department has its own rules about which patients residents examine and treat, and under what circumstances. Although patients have the right to refuse the care of a resident (or any other staff member), they are discouraged from doing so. In anesthesiology, where all the faces are unfamiliar, a woman will usually not even know if she is being treated by a resident.

Institutions also have financial interests to protect. In order to provide a wide range of services and to keep up with technological advances, they need a substantial income stream. On the one hand, this makes the hospital eager to satisfy patients so they'll speak highly of their experience to other potential patients. On the other hand, the hospital also wants to see that the equipment and services for which it can bill are used to capacity. In our fee-for-service system, every IV placed, every pill dispensed, and every monitor connected bring extra income into the hospital. Similarly, every administration of anesthesia brings extra income into the anesthesia service. Financial interests may also make the hospital willing to keep an incompetent, impaired, or unscrupulous doctor who brings in a steady stream of patients, rather than relieve him of his privileges to practice there.

The hospital's legal interests also figure in its reluctance to discharge objectionable practitioners. Litigiousness is not restricted to patients. A doctor who is relieved of hospital privileges is likely to sue the hospital for interfering with his livelihood. Unless the evidence is clear in the records (it usually isn't since the doctor writes them) or enough witnesses testify in court, the hospital will lose the case. Worse off than before, it will have to take back the offending physician and probably pay damages. Increasingly, hospitals are finding it necessary to employ full-time legal counsels public-relations officers, and "patient advocates," to protect their concerns and reputations in the community, the press, the courts, and the legislature.

The point of these remarks is not to deny the dedication of individual doctors, nurses, childbirth instructors, and hospital administrators, but rather to help you understand how the constraints under which they collectively function may influence your care. You should be aware of the inevitably diverse interests that are involved in obstetrics and make arrangements that realistically take these into account. A simple fact of life is that you can count on people to serve your best interests if they see these as also being in their own interests or at least not in conflict with their own interests. Other arrangements are not reliable and should be avoided or neutralized. You can avoid most problems by choosing care providers who are personally committed to supportive obstetrical care (see Chapters 9 and 10). Residual problems may be neutralized by the support of a private labor assistant and a strategy of congenial evasion (see Chapter 12).

9

HOSPITALITY

THE physical and psychological parameters of your birth experience are determined to a very large extent by the setting you choose. Even in a small community there is usually more than one hospital within a reasonable distance. A careful choice is important because the policies of the obstetrics department, the facilities of the labor and delivery unit, and the attitude of the staff limit the range of options available to you and your obstetrician. It is part of your obstetrician's job to see that you get the best his hospital has to offer and are protected from the worst. But, as we have just seen, there are limits to what your obstetrician can do, especially during those parts of labor when he is not actually present. *Before* interviewing a doctor, you should therefore know as much as possible about the hospital he uses. Familiarity with his working environment will help you to focus your questions, evaluate his answers, and, in the process, bolster your self-confidence.

In conjunction with other aspects of childbirth education, hospitals generally offer prospective parents tours of their maternity facilities—admitting office, labor and delivery unit, postpartum areas, and nurseries. Conducted late in pregnancy, like the childbirth classes themselves, these tours are designed to familiarize patients with the hospital so that they will feel more comfortable and cooperative when they arrive. The assumption is that the expectant parents have already chosen a physician who uses that hospital and that they are reasonably content with the choice.

Although the tours are not intended to be used as shopping expeditions, they can and should be adapted for that purpose by arranging them as early as possible. When you call the hospital to schedule a tour, you are likely to be asked when your due date is and who your doctor is. If your due date is far off (or not yet existent), you can say that you want to learn more about the hospital in order to inform your choice of a doctor. Most maternity staff will cooperate. If they don't, that tells you something about the hospital already. Although you may be the least pregnant person in the tour group, you will be in the best position to use the information you get and will probably be (perhaps grudgingly) admired for it. If possible, you should visit several hospitals and at least one free-standing birth center in order to have a solid basis for comparison. In evaluating each, you should refer to your childbirth protocol (Chapter 7). Ask yourself: "What will it take to get the kind of care I want in this place? Is it possible at all? Will I need to make special arrangements to obtain what I think I need?" Your hospital visits may in turn suggest worthwhile changes in your protocol.

Because creature comforts are important for a smooth labor, the labor and delivery unit should be evaluated at the first level like a hotel. Start by noting how you are received. If a hotel manager were to greet you with the attitude "We're glad to see you, and we hope you'll make yourself at home," you would feel welcome and at ease. If he were to greet you with "You're lucky to get into this citadel, and we hope you won't give us any trouble," you would feel unwelcome and uneasy. The same applies to a hospital.

Next, you should note whether the facilities are adequate for the activities you plan. Is there a pleasant space to wander around in early labor? Are the labor rooms dominated by the bed and other paraphernalia, or spacious enough for a mobile, active labor, with mate on one side and assistant on the other? Are the labor rooms equipped to be used legally as birthing rooms, or are births officially expected to take place in the delivery (operating) room? Is a portable commode with hand rails available to support a semistanding position in the second stage? Are three pillows available per patient, or will you need to bring your own?

Is the bed low enough and wide enough? Is there a toilet close by and a shower readily available? Is the lighting adjustable and the privacy (acoustical as well as visual) adequate?

After noting the facilities, you should pay close attention to the staff. These strangers, rather than your hand-picked familiar doctor, are the ones who will be responsible for your care during most of your labor. In virtually all cultures, mothers in labor are normally attended by women. In traditional societies these women are midwives trained through experience to see most births to a safe conclusion with strong support and minimal intervention. In technological societies women in labor are usually attended by obstetrical nurses, who have little or no training in midwifery skills and who are expected to defer to doctors in the management of labor and the mechanics of delivery. Those maternity units in the technological world with low rates of medical delivery are the ones with exceptionally high proportions of midwives on their staffs. Like all of us, attendants use the protocols they know, and only midwives are trained thoroughly in alternatives to conventional obstetrics. Recognizing this, the chief of obstetrics in one of Harvard's major teaching hospitals says (privately) that he wishes he could replace all the attending physicians in his labor and delivery unit with midwives.

In the Netherlands, the midwives are the respected authorities on normal labor and delivery and are responsible for instructing physicians in this area. In this country, doctors receive little training or experience in normal labor and delivery at all. The sensitive ones have learned by carefully listening to and observing their patients. Recently our maternity nurses have begun to receive training in midwifery skills. Nurse-midwifery programs produce graduates who may deliver babies with rules for supervision, backup, and intervention that vary according to state laws and hospital policy. During your hospital tour you should ask what kinds of training the nursing staff have received, how autonomously they function, and what philosophies of childbirth support and management they subscribe to. If the answers sound nice but vague, ask for specific examples of things that the nurses will try to do for patients and how they might respond to special requests like those in your pro-

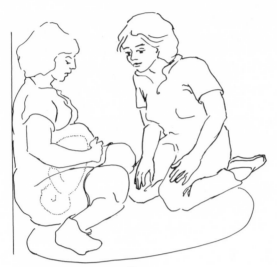

FIGURE 11. CREATIVE USE
OF HOSPITAL FURNISHINGS

A. Even a wall can provide
   useful support.
B. A portable commode can
   be used as a birthing chair
   or to support a standing
   squat.

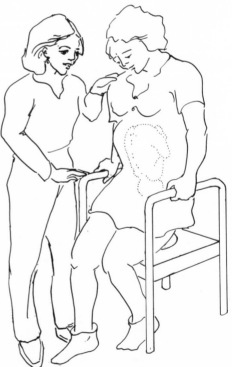

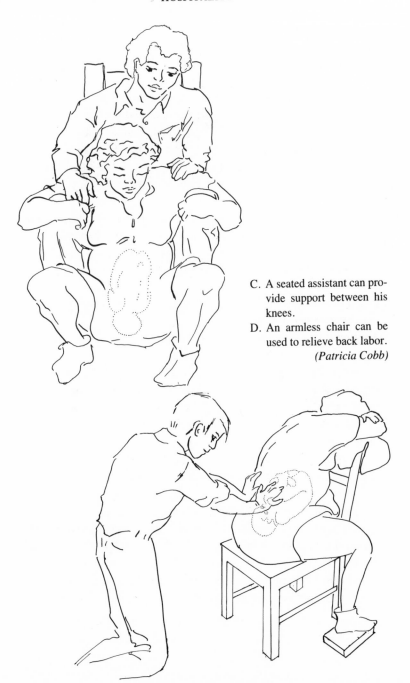

C. A seated assistant can provide support between his knees.
D. An armless chair can be used to relieve back labor.

(Patricia Cobb)

tocol. The number of mothers a nurse is responsible for at any one time and the continuity of support the nurse provides during active labor are also important indicators of the quality of nursing care.

The quality of obstetric anesthesiology may also vary a great deal from hospital to hospital. To evaluate the anesthesiology service, ask what attitudes prevail there regarding unmedicated birth and regional anesthesia for surgical birth. Check also whether an anesthesiologist is always in the hospital or only on call. This coverage affects the promptness with which emergencies can be handled. If anesthesiologists routinely see all patients, you should find out what they will do or ask and whether the visit can be waived. If the hospital is a teaching hospital, residents and medical students may be involved in your care. You should ask how residents are assigned and what role they play relative to the nurses and your own doctor. In general, it is also useful to know what action you are advised to take if you are uncomfortable with any staff member.

In addition to assessing the physical facilities and the staff, you need to become familiar with the unit's policies. For example, you should find out what rules govern eating and drinking in labor. Some hospitals (including a few prestigious teaching hospitals) have begun to encourage moderate eating and drinking. Some others will overlook it, although it is against official policy. However, many rigidly enforce *nihil per os* or allow only ice chips. You should also ask what the standard policy is in regard to pharmacological augmentation of labor. Are limits of time imposed on the length of any stage of labor before or after membranes rupture? In the same vein, you should ask about the policies for IVs, enemas, preps, monitors, the use of your own clothes, birth in the labor room, and sustained contact with the baby in the minutes and hours immediately following birth. If you have had previous uterine surgery, you should ask what extra restrictions of time, place, or prophylaxis, if any, will be imposed on your labor. Some hospitals require women with this history to have IVs, be monitored continuously, and give birth in the delivery room. If you have older children, close extended family, or special friends, you may want them to be able to attend the birth. In this case, you will need to know what rules (as well as space considerations) govern their presence. Some hospitals exclude private labor assistants or severely restrict their activities. Even if you have decided against employing one, the option is a vital sign of the hospital's interest in supportive obstetrics.

As a measure of the effectiveness of the overall efforts of the unit, you should ask for the hospital's rates of cesarean delivery (broken down into primary and repeat), instrumental delivery (broken down into low, mid, and high), and various forms of anesthesia and analgesia. These statistics will form a basis for comparing hospitals with each other, and the practices of individual doctors with those of others working at the same hospital. Cesarean rates should not be above 20 percent (roughly 14 percent primary and 6 percent repeat) and should preferably be below 10 percent (roughly 7 percent primary and 3 percent repeat). Instrumental delivery (forceps and suction cap) should not be above 15 percent and should preferably be below 5 percent. Among these there should be no high extractions and only rare mid-extractions. The use of pain medication (anesthesia and analgesia) should not be above 50 percent and should preferably be below 15 percent; the latter indicates that it is largely restricted to operative deliveries. Among the medicated births, general anesthesia should be rare.

Hospitals with high rates of medical delivery and anesthesia may blame them on a relatively high-risk patient population. However, the experience of the North Central Bronx Hospital and the Booth Memorial Maternity Center has shown that excellent outcomes can be obtained in a high-risk patient population with very little medical intervention of any kind (see Chapter 3). Except for women with serious medical conditions (e.g., heart disease) who are generally referred to specialists at specially equipped and staffed tertiary care centers, and women with unambiguous obstetrical emergencies (e.g., *placentae previa* or *abruptio placentae*), high-risk mothers and babies benefit as much as or more than others from supportive noninterventionist care. If your tour guide does not know the hospital's statistics, she should be able to tell you where in the hospital to inquire. It should not be necessary for you to go (or threaten to go) to the state hospital accreditation board to get these numbers. However, if you suspect that the information you are given is inaccurate, you may want to check with the state authorities.

Following your visit to the labor and delivery unit, you will probably be shown the postpartum area and nurseries. This is a good time to inquire about policies concerning neonatal procedures. To begin with, ask what criteria are used for inserting a breathing tube or sending the baby immediately to the nursery. If the hospital is not a tertiary care center, in-house services will be limited. In this case, find out under what circumstances a baby would be transferred to another hospital, to which hospital he would be transferred, and whether you would also be transferred. With regard to routine procedures, ask first whether they can be postponed until the baby's first alert period for bonding (one to two hours) is over. The baby's general health can be observed (and an Apgar score can be given) while he is in your arms. Washing and weighing are not urgent matters and can be done as convenient. Eye treatment for prevention of gonorrheal infection interferes with vision[1] and should be postponed until the baby is sleepy. (In some places it may be possible to waive the eye treatment altogether on the basis of a negative gonorrhea culture shortly before birth, the confidence of both the mother and her mate that there has been no exposure to gonorrhea, or the pediatrician's intention to examine the infant's eyes for signs of infection a few days after birth so that any necessary treatment can be given before damage occurs.) Some tests (e.g., for PKU and jaundice) and shots (e.g., of vitamin K) may also be routine. Ask which these are, what the tests involve, and what the purpose of the shots is.

Since you are unlikely to need to stay in the postpartum area more than twenty-four hours unless you've had a cesarean delivery or a particularly difficult vaginal delivery, you should base your evaluation of this part of the hospital on its support for cesarean mothers. Ask specifically what special help is provided to cesarean mothers. Is ambulation within the day and a normal diet within a few days encouraged? Is help provided with handling the baby, including breast feeding? Is rooming-in flexible to accommodate both the need for contact and the need for rest? Are electric pumps available for the mother whose baby is too weak to suck, in order to establish milk production for the baby's present and future needs? Are visiting privileges as limited or as liberal as you would like, to balance the need for rest with the need for the support of family and friends? Can older siblings have physical contact with both mother and newborn for reassurance and bonding? Are private rooms available so you can get enough rest? If you share a room, can you get a roommate who is also a nonsmoker if you are or who has had a cesarean delivery if you have?

Before leaving the hospital you should try to talk privately with the tour leader and the personnel in the labor and delivery unit. Meeting the L&D staff is especially important if the tour leader is a public-relations officer or a childbirth instructor rather than one of the medical staff. At this time you can ask what special advice they have for getting the kind of care you want in their unit. You can find out whether they would like to have a written list of your preferences. Although the staff cannot tell you which doctors are "good" or "bad," they can tell you which doctors have a "style" of practice most consistent with your preferences. They can tell you who practices "traditional" or "old-fashioned" obstetrics (often euphemisms for out-of-date obstetrics), who practices modern technological (i.e., interventionist) obstetrics, and who practices supportive noninterventionist obstetrics. They may also be able to tell you about private labor assistants who have worked in their unit. This information, from people who have observed doctors and labor assistants in action, is particularly valuable. It is also useful to ask staff members how they would compare their maternity unit with others in the area. Their responses will tell you what they regard as their greatest strengths and their competitors greatest weaknesses. The competition, of course, will tell you the other side of the story. Balanced against each other, these perspectives can help you interpret your own observations and identify important issues.

The tour may not address all your concerns. In this case, you should not hesitate to phone the head nurse of the labor and delivery unit (or the head nurse of the entire maternity unit) either to ask questions directly or to arrange an appointment for a more extended conversation. If she is sympathetic, this woman can tell you how she feels about her nursing staff: its training, its commitment, its range of viewpoints, its responsiveness, and its constraints. She can comment on your childbirth protocol and indicate what you and she can do to assure that it is followed. She can tell you what rules are flexible and how to work around them, which doctors have styles of practice most consistent with your preferences, and how to locate a good labor assistant. If she is not sympathetic, that too tells you a lot about the hospital.

Following each hospital visit, make a list of your positive and negative impressions for your future reference. An example of such a list is given below. It is based on the preferences in childbirth management delineated in Chapters 3 through 7. It assumes (I hope correctly, but you should check) that all hospitals in this country now allow fathers to be present at all births (vaginal and surgical) and give them round-the-clock visiting privileges afterward. In each hospital some mix of good and bad features is to be expected. You will need to decide which of these, in combination with which attendants, will work best for you.

IMPRESSIONS OF HOSPITALITY

Bad Signs	*Good Signs*
Registration (completion of admission and financial forms) must be done at the time of arrival. Parents are advised to leave home early to allow extra time for this or to have the father register while the mother goes alone to L&D.	Registration can be done well in advance.
The décor is beautiful, but the staff are brisk and discouraging, all "business."	The décor may be a bit shabby, but the staff are warm and encouraging.

94

HOSPITALITY

Bad Signs   *Good Signs*

Private labor assistants are not
allowed.

Private labor assistants are welcome.

It is the hospital's policy for patients
in labor to have nothing by mouth
but antacid.

It is the hospital's policy to encourage women in labor to eat and drink
lightly.

The bed and equipment completely
dominate the labor room. There is so
little space around the bed that if I
want to get out of it, one of my com-
panions will have to get in!

There is plenty of space in the labor
room for pacing and for squatting,
with an assistant on each side.

The delivery room has a space-age
one-size-fits-all plastic molded
"birthing chair" (the kind where the
doctor controls the height and tilt),
and the staff want every patient to
use it.

The labor rooms have beds that break
away into "birthing chairs" (the kind
where the mother controls the position of the back and footrests). But
the staff are just as happy if mothers
choose to stand or squat on the floor.

The nurses complain that it is hard
to keep track of mothers who wander around.

The nurses encourage walking in
labor.

The chief of obstetrics says the argu-
ments against the use of Pitocin and
forceps are controversial.

The chief of obstetrics actively discourages the use of Pitocin and forceps.

The policy is that mothers with any
previous uterine surgery must have
an IV, must be monitored continuously, may labor for only a limited
time, and must give birth in the
delivery room.

The policy is that mothers with previous uterine surgery (in the lower
segment) are to be treated like mothers with no such surgery except for
special attention paid to blood pressure.

NEGOTIATING SUPPORTIVE OBSTETRICAL CARE

Bad Signs	*Good Signs*
The anesthesiologists in this hospital give heavy epidurals and don't allow them to wear off for pushing.	The anesthesiologists in this hospital give very light epidurals and allow them to wear off for pushing.
Continuous electronic monitoring is encouraged in all cases.	Electronic monitoring is reserved for risky situations and then used intermittently, if possible.
IVs are routine and run continuously.	IVs are used only when and as long as necessary.
The cesarean rate is high, and the chief of obstetrics is unconcerned.	The cesarean rate is moderate, and the chief of obstetrics is trying to bring it down.
The baby's siblings are not admitted to L&D.	Siblings may come and go at will during a vaginal birth, if the mother is comfortable with their presence and the children are under supervision.
Siblings may visit with mother in the lounge and hallway and see the baby through the nursery glass.	Siblings may visit with mother and baby in their postpartum room.
Residents do an admissions examination on all patients and are expected to place orders for IVs and monitors.	Residents are not involved with private patients except at the request of the personal physician (e.g., to assist in surgery).
The anesthesiologist interviews all patients shortly after admission. The interview cannot be waived.	The anesthesiologist sees mothers only upon request.
Most of the labor rooms and postpartum rooms are multiple-bed.	All of the labor rooms and most of the postpartum rooms are private.

HOSPITALITY

Bad Signs

Good Signs

Routine neonatal procedures are done in the nursery while the mother is still in L&D.

Routine neonatal procedures are done at the mother's bedside, usually after she is settled in her postpartum room.

The delivery room is used for all births except those that happen too fast to get there.

The delivery room is used only for cesarean births.

A couple of midwives tried to practice at this hospital a few years ago, but they gave up within a few months.

In this hospital, more births are attended by midwives than by obstetricians.

10

GUARDIAN ANGEL OR
KNIGHT ON A HIGH HORSE?

THE most important part of negotiating supportive obstetrical care is choosing the right physician. But this is also generally the most difficult part. Interviewing a doctor can be expensive, tricky, and emotionally taxing. To be successful you must adopt a stance relative to authority and expertise that few of us have been taught or encouraged to take. This is why I recommend that you first build up your knowledge and confidence with extensive reading and hospital visits. These should help you develop a clear idea of what you're looking for, how to justify it, and how it compares with standard practice.

Hopefully, the first part of this book has convinced you that conventional high-tech obstetrics undermines natural childbirth and that you don't want it practiced on you and your baby. But what is the alternative? If a doctor doesn't do what he was taught to do, what does he do? Few doctors actually provide labor support or assistance themselves. They are not trained to, usually don't have the time or the temperament for it, and rarely feel free to establish the closeness with the patient that is needed to do a good job. In some cases they may actively encourage good labor support by suggesting that patients engage experienced assistants or by calling the nurse's attention to the patient's needs, preferences, and expectations. However, at the very least the doctor should keep himself and others from getting in the way of good labor support.

Specifically, your doctor should protect you from aggressive residents, anesthesiologists, and nurses. He himself should avoid unnecessary prophylaxis, minimize environmental disturbances, and resist the ever-present temptation to tamper. He should be prepared to put the skills of his trade to work in your behalf if nature double-crosses you but otherwise leave the job to those who can do it better. He should not be disappointed if he has nothing more to do than hover observantly nearby, take notes, and maybe (or maybe not) catch the baby. He should draw his satisfaction from the fulfillment of the strengths of his patients rather than the extent to which he has an active role in their births.

If your doctor thinks intervention should be considered, he should explain what and why. Except in the rare emergency that requires rapid action, he should also explain the possible side effects of the proposed intervention and how these will be handled. Then he should give you plenty of time (three contractions worth at the absolute minimum) and privacy (his absence) to discuss with your mate and/or labor assistant what you want to do. All of this takes a good deal of patience, humility, caring, tolerance, sensitivity, and humor, qualities that are not particularly cultivated in medical training. Noting that "Doctors say they deliver babies and midwives say they attend births," a Harvard professor of obstetrics admonishes doctors "to do less delivering and more attending." Others say more graphically that "an obstetrician should have a broad behind and the good sense to know when to sit on it."

How do you find this angel? By now you should be well on your way. During your hospital tours you have obtained the names of doctors who experienced people think will suit your preferences. You also may have the names of labor assistants you can contact for recommendations of doctors who are skilled in obstetrical technology but very restrained in its use. Other sources of referrals are childbirth educators, La Leche League leaders, and friends. However, be cautious about the advice you receive. A friend may think her doctor was wonderful because he gave her pain medication at the first groan and convinced her that his episiotomy saved her sex life (or at least her husband's). If someone recommends her physician to you, ask specifically what she liked about him and why. To find out how supportive he is, ask how they communicated before and during labor about choices in childbirth. To find out how interventionist he is, ask which part of her labor she spent in bed and why, in what position she delivered and why, whether she had an episiotomy and if so how and when it was justified to her. Ask whether pain medication was used and if so when and why, whether labor was augmented pharmacologically or surgically and if so when and why, and how comfortable she felt physically and psychologically postpartum. It would also be helpful to know what, if anything, she would do differently if she had it to do again. You might find the answers surprising, if not shocking.

Once you have a list of likely candidates for your guardian angel, how do you choose which ones to interview? By calling their offices and checking the *Directory of Medical Specialists* in your local library you can learn more about their training, their ages, their special medical interests, the hospitals they use, and the structure of their practices. You might prefer a younger doctor to whom you can relate as a peer or an older doctor whose distance from your social circle makes you feel less self-conscious. Obstetrics is rapidly changing, and physicians can easily grow obsolete. But some older physicians have kept up to date and may be much more comfortable with supportive care than young doctors who have only known high-tech obstetrics.

You also may prefer a female doctor to a male doctor. Other things being equal, you may be more comfortable discussing physical and emotional aspects of reproductive health with a female doctor. If she has herself given birth and has a philosophy similar to yours, she may be ideally empathetic. On the other hand, a man who appreciates that he will never really know what it is like to give birth may be more tolerant of different approaches. As a man in our culture, he may also better understand the appeal of a physical challenge and the rewards of physical effort. Doctors of both sexes, of course, can be equally unable to shake the cultural prejudice that physical effort (not to mention the enjoyment of it) does not become a woman.

Another important consideration is the composition of the doctor's practice. Ideally you would like a doctor with enough experience in low-risk births to feel comfortable taking a back-seat role but with enough experience with complications to be skilled in diagnosing and treating them. Unless you have a medical condition that specifically places you or your baby at high risk, you should not choose a high-risk specialist as your doctor. These obstetricians sometimes have cesarean rates as high as 90 percent and little confidence in natural birthing mechanisms. In general, it is also unwise to choose a doctor whose practice is primarily gynecologic. Spontaneous complications warranting medical intervention (as opposed to physicians' mistakes requiring medical rescue) occur in only about 10 percent of an average population of patients. A doctor attending fewer than one hundred births a year will have fewer than ten opportunities to refresh his skills in the diagnosis and treatment of such complications, unless he intervenes unnecessarily in some of his patients' births. Although all rules have their exceptions, you should be particularly wary of the doctors whose practices consist heavily of gynecology or high-risk obstetric referrals. Instead, concentrate your search among doctors who have developed active primary obstetrics practices.

It is extremely important to find out from the doctor's receptionist how he divides his time and who acts as his backup. In general, patients get better attention if the practice is restricted to one office and one hospital. The doctor is not helping anyone while he is running all around town. If he has a completely solo practice (i.e., no nurse practitioner, midwife, or fellow obstetrician with whom to share call), it is vital that his office be inside or very close to the hospital, so that he can go back and forth easily between the office and the labor and delivery unit. This minimizes the temptation to push patients in labor in order to meet office appointments. It will also be necessary to check that the backup that the doctor considers compatible with his interests is also compatible with yours. If he is in a duo practice, you should find out whether the doctors alternate office hours and call hours, so that one doctor can always cover the needs of hospital patients without concern about the office schedule or his next night's sleep. Again, you will need to find out if the second doctor also suits your preferences adequately. If the practice is larger, it will be more difficult to negotiate good care with confidence. How will you get to know (much less like and trust) all the doctors? How will they get to know (and like and trust) you? And how will you be able to get that many people to agree to any one way of managing labor? In a large practice you and your baby will have to take your chances.

Once you have found out as much as you can from those peripheral to the doctor himself, you are ready to schedule an interview. In making an appointment, you should make it *very* clear that you are only interested in meeting the doctor and learning more about his practices. If routine bloods, urines, weights, blood pressures, etc. are taken, and/or if an examination is done, you will have to pay for these as well as the interview itself. In terms of interviewing strategy, it is best not to push the doctor into a corner. You might begin by saying that you have come to see him because you have heard X and Y, which appeals to you. This gives you the opportunity to verify the impressions you have gained from others while giving him a positive sense of what you are looking for. You can also tell him what you liked best about the hospital he uses, to see whether he agrees.

As the conversation progresses, you should find out how he feels about such matters as pain medication, eating in labor, private labor assistants, episiotomies, fetal monitoring, and labor augmentation. If the answers are vague, ask him what proportions of his patients have no pain medication, no labor stimulation, and no episiotomy. Ask also what his rates of cesarean and instrumental delivery are. If he does not know these rates (approximately), that is a sign that neither he nor his hospital chief care enough to monitor his practices properly. If he knows these rates but is unwilling to discuss them with you, that is a very serious sign of unresponsiveness. At some point you should also be sure to find out what standing orders he gives the hospital, if any, and when and how he involves residents in intrapartum and postpartum care. If you have concerns about the facilities, staff, or policies of the hospital he uses, ask what he or you can do about them. If you've had previous uterine surgery, you should find out what difference he feels this makes in the way your labor should be monitored and evaluated. Before leaving, you should also find out how he thinks his backup's answers to your questions would differ from his.

Throughout the conversation you should feel free to ask the doctor to explain any unfamiliar terminology and the basis (including literature references) for any strongly held opinions. In general, your approach can be assertive without being aggressive—firm and persistent, if need be, but in a friendly and an understanding, rather than a hostile, manner. Like anyone else, a doctor will not respond well if put on the defensive. On the other hand, you should not be put on the defensive either. When you ask a question you should expect an answer, not a reprimand. Unless accompanied by a thoughtful and thorough explanation, responses like "It's for your safety" and "You must think of your baby" are gratuitous, evasive, and insulting. So, too, are responses like "No one else has ever asked that," "You seem to have trouble accepting advice," and "Why don't you let me worry about those things." You should never feel compelled to apologize for your questions. In this situation it is best to emphasize that you are willing to be persuaded by a convincing explanation. If this doesn't work, it's the doctor's problem, not yours. Some doctors will feel threatened by any questions, no matter how diplomatically presented. This insecurity usually matches their ignorance and incompetence. It is a warning sign that should be taken very seriously.

In conducting the interview, you should realize that doctors usually charge according to the time taken. In general, what you want for your money at this stage is to find out what his preferences (and his backup's) are and whether these are flexible. You can't possibly cover all contingencies. What you can do is get a general sense of whether this doctor is *supportive,* so that you can expect him to encourage you in labor, and *communicative,* so that you can expect him to solicit your informed participation in decisions. It is not important at this point for you to tell him any more about what you know or want than is necessary to gauge his reaction. If the conversation gets derailed, try to bring it back to the point, bluntly if necessary. If you reach an impasse, thank him for his time and interest, and leave. You can be sincerely grateful if he has been candid in his objections to your preferences because this is the best time to find these out. The real problem is the doctor who strings you along with disingenuous or outright deceitful answers, or who allows himself to get involved in a style of practice with which he is not comfortable and which he ultimately cannot carry off. In fact, it is important that you respect the doctor's integrity and preferences as much as you want him to respect yours. Although you have the ultimate right to accept or refuse interventions, it is a great mistake to overestimate a doctor's willingness or ability to adapt to your preferences. If, for example, a doctor is afraid to do without electronic monitoring, then his nervousness may make you uneasy and/or he may look for excuses to start it. In the end, neither of you will be happy. On the other hand, a doctor who doesn't approve of routine continuous monitoring and does it only for legal protection may welcome the patient who relieves him of this constraint by specifically requesting that it not be used.

In evaluating your visit, consider the entire impression. Start with the waiting room. Was the wait reasonable? If not, was there an apology? What kind of literature was available while you waited? Different types of magazines indicate the expectation of different types of clientele. Do you fit into the range of expectations expressed here? Is literature on women's health also available, and, if so, does it represent a point of view consonant with yours?

Next consider how you are received. Has the doctor selected a competent and friendly staff? Are they accustomed to patient interviews, or do they assume you're in for an examination? Does the doctor introduce himself warmly? Does his office feel friendly or very imposing? Are the chairs miles apart or at a conversational distance? Does the doctor welcome questions and even try to anticipate them, or is he defensive, suspicious, condescending, or outright hostile? Do his answers make sense? Are they pitched at the level you addressed or obscured with excessive and intimidating technical jargon? Is he interested in knowing what you've read, or is he disdainful of and closed to new information and ideas? Does he respect your efforts to learn about obstetrics or feel threatened by them? Does he suggest other things you might read? Does he offer the names of labor assistants and childbirth educators that he recommends? Above all, do you feel comfortable talking to him?

Trust your gut reaction. Unfortunately, individuals who are otherwise good judges of human character often suspend judgment when it comes to physicians and accept behavior from them that they would not accept from anyone else. If anything, you should be especially critical of individuals entrusted with your health and that of your baby. Keep in mind that when you give a doctor the benefit of the doubt, you are taking it away from yourself. You will find that it is easy to recognize supportive obstetricians because they stand out in a profession that tends to breed arrogance. Traditionally, physicians believe (1) that patients will lose confidence in a doctor who appears less than certain of what is best, (2) that a doctor has failed in a central part of his job if he cannot convince his patient of the objective wisdom of standard practices (never mind that last year's were different and next year's probably will be too), and (3) that psychological and social concerns are separable from and less important than physical ones. When a doctor subscribes to these views, informed consent becomes a charade. You should not hesitate to reject such an outdated style of practice.[1] His years of schooling should not give him any special status in your life. You hire him as a source of specialized information, to be available as the need arises, and as a technician with pertinent skills, to be employed at your discretion. A physician, like anyone else, is entitled to your respect, but an unfamiliar physician should neither expect nor be given more trust than any other stranger. Trust (and hopefully friendship) is earned with time.

It is essential that you make the effort to interview more than one physician. This gives you a useful basis for comparison. It also gives you the security of having a familiar doctor to turn to if your first choice falls through for some reason. As pregnancy goes on, you will get to know your doctor and his backup better, and they will get to know you better. Either party may decide that they made a mistake. Although doctors cannot legally or ethically abandon a patient abruptly once care has started, they can, with sufficient notice, ask you to find other care providers. Even if they don't, it is not in your best interest to continue with doctors who do not feel comfortable with you. Nor is it wise for you to continue with doctors who make you uncomfortable. If this situation should arise, it is much easier to change if you already have a familiar place to go.

It is also helpful to have a familiar place to go if you want a second opinion during your pregnancy. Prenatal diagnostic procedures are being recommended with increasing frequency in spite of concerns about their safety, the accuracy of the results, and the appropriate uses of the information obtained. A second opinion can help to sort out the controversies and their relevance to your particular situation. Indeed, women have been known to change obstetricians after their due date as a result of disagreement over the handling of "postmaturity" issues (e.g., the conduct and interpretation of stress and nonstress tests, and the induction of labor). With a quick phone call and car ride, women have also changed doctors and hospitals in early labor (e.g., when their doctor has sent in an unfamiliar substitute or when disagreements have arisen about labor augmentation and fasting). In order to have these options, you need to know more than one acceptable care provider. If you box yourself into a corner at the outset by prematurely committing yourself to one group of obstetricians, you risk finding yourself trapped in the end.

One important test of your chosen doctor, short of the birth itself, will be the history and first exam. You can learn a great deal about his sensitivity and thoroughness from his conduct at this time. The history should be taken in the doctor's office when you are fully clothed. The questions should be detailed but respectful. He should be interested in your life style (nutrition, exercise, work, stress) as well as your medical background. His estimation of the baby's "due date" should take into account any knowledge you might have the timing of conception (e.g., a tendency to long menstrual cycles indicative of delayed ovulation, the use or nonuse of contraception, and periods of sexual abstinence related to travel or other factors). Throughout, the doctor should be attentive. Both you and he should recognize that examinations, clinical chemistry, and diagnostic technology are no substitutes for your knowledge of your own body. During your discussion, he should not avoid your gaze or vice versa. If you find yourself looking away, consider what is the source of your discomfort and what you can do to relieve it. If it is the doctor who is talking to the desk or the window, you can tell him that you are finding it hard to follow what he is saying when he is not making eye contact, and see if that helps.

In the examining room you should not be left waiting spread-eagle for the doctor to come in, but rather greet him sitting upright or standing. The exam should be gentle and thorough (without unnecessary lingering). Unless there is something wrong, the pelvic exam should not be painful. Tense abdominal and pelvic muscles cause unnecessary discomfort for you and difficulty for the doctor. The doctor should therefore notice any muscle tension and give you a chance to relax. If he doesn't, you should tell him that the exam is uncomfortable and note whether he makes an effort to slow down, be less rough, and/or use more lubricant. If he blames you for being tense or is otherwise uncooperative, you'd best get off the table, collect your things, and leave (using the bathroom to change back into your clothes). Ideally, the doctor should explain what he's checking for, how you can expect it to feel, and what he finds. If there is anything interesting to see (e.g., cervical changes), it is thoughtful for him to show it to you with a mirror; and if there is anything interesting to feel, it is thoughtful for him to help you locate it with your fingers (e.g., the fundus in early pregnancy and the parts of the baby in late pregnancy). When a metal speculum is used, it should be warmed first. For a pap smear, the cervix should be scraped with a light touch (no jabbing). Although it is less important, socks covering the cold metal stirrups also indicate an interest in your comfort.

Another good test of your chosen doctor is your mate's first visit. Some obstetricians are noticeably more deferential to men than to their patients. You should be certain that the doctor appreciates that his primary responsibility is to you. He should introduce himself to your mate the same way he does to you (whether that be with title or by first name), and he should answer your mate's questions with the same degree of interest and specificity that he does yours. You should always feel that you are part of the discussion rather than just its subject.

Considering all the facets of human interaction involved, it is obviously unlikely that any one group of doctors will be perfect for you. However, when you compromise, it is best to do so with a clear understanding of just what it is you are giving up. You should consider the good and bad features of different practice groups and which faults are easiest for you to live with or compensate for. Examples of common good and bad signs are listed below. You will probably regard some of these as serious, others as trivial, and perhaps some even as the reverse of what you prefer. (Lest some of the bad signs seem exaggerated, let me assure you they are all based on real cases.) In considering the choices available to you, you should pick the doctor who best meets your most serious needs, and hope that over the course of your prenatal visits you will reach greater rapport in other areas.

IMPRESSIONS OF ANGEL POTENTIAL

Bad Signs	*Good Signs*
Dr. Knight says he does X when he thinks it is necessary.	Dr. Angel says that if he thinks X would help, he will let us know and (except in a rare emergency) expect us to take time to discuss it and think about it.
Dr. K. says he discusses birth-management options with patients later in pregnancy, when it is more relevant.	Dr. A. says we should discuss my childbirth preferences early so we can decide if we are right for each other and relax.
Dr. K. says my wishes are all well and good, but I should keep an open mind.	Dr. A. says he will do what he can to help me get what I want.

Bad Signs	*Good Signs*
Dr. K. says women are not hungry in labor, so it is not necessary to discuss eating.	Dr. A. says that if I am hungry in labor, that's a sign that I need to eat.
It seems that whenever I ask Dr. K. to explain something, he says that it is his job to worry about all these things.	Dr. A. said that I should ask all the questions that occur to me so I will have more confidence in the process and be able to make well-informed decisions.
Dr. K. says that he uses oxytocin "to get it over with."	Dr. A. says that he puts no limit of time on any stage of labor if the baby and mother are holding up well.
Dr. K. says that he isn't comfortable delivering a baby on the floor.	Dr. A. says he can adjust to whatever birth position works best for me.
Dr. K. says that the baby will fall on the floor if I give birth upright.	Dr. A. says that the baby can't fall as far if I'm on my feet as it can if I'm up on a table and that if I squat we can just let the baby slide out onto a pad on the floor.
When I complained about discomfort during the pelvic exam, Dr. K. said, "If you can't take this, you'll never make it through natural childbirth."	Dr. A. explained what he was looking for in the pelvic exam and how relaxing my muscles made the exam easier for both of us. He also explained that relaxing these muscles in labor would make the birth easier.
Dr. K. says that he recommends what he would want for himself or his wife.	Dr. A. says women do best in labor when their individual preferences are taken into account.

109

Bad Signs	*Good Signs*
Dr. K. dismisses inhibition of labor by monitors and IVs as a ''social issue.''	Dr. A. says that monitors and IVs should only be used with specific indications because they inhibit labor. He also says that mothers should receive extra attention and encouragement when they need to be on monitors or IVs.
Dr. K. says that I have to trust him.	Dr. A. says that he hopes that we'll come to trust one another.
Dr. K. says that I'm letting my hedonism interfere with my baby's welfare and that we can't take chances.	Dr. A. says that there is no way that is risk-free but that, unless there are serious problems, the best way is the one in which I can work most effectively.
Dr. K. didn't discuss nutrition in pregnancy. He just handed me a prenatal vitamin prescription.	Dr. A. discussed the importance of good nutrition for the development of the baby and for the prevention of birth complications.
Dr. K. considers home birth dangerous.	Dr. A. provides backup to qualified midwives attending properly screened home births.
Dr. K. gave my friend an episiotomy without any warning beforehand or explanation afterward, even though she had told him that she didn't want one.	Dr. A. told my friend that her baby would be born in about ten more pushes with no episiotomy and about five more pushes with an episiotomy and that the choice was up to her.
Dr. K. says that the increase in cesarean births in recent years has produced better babies.	Dr. A. says that the increase in cesarean deliveries in recent years may have improved outcomes for

Bad Signs   *Good Signs*

low-birth-weight infants which are
most common in adverse maternal
circumstances, but that no improvement has been proven for babies of
well-nourished, healthy mothers.

Dr. K. says that in his experience X   Dr. A. says that most routine inter-
is beneficial.   ventions are of such marginal benefit, if any, that they cannot be
evaluated without a proper statistical
study of a population of patients
larger than in any one doctor's practice.

Dr. K. says that the hospital requires   Dr. A says that the hospital requires
birth in the delivery room in my case.   birth in the delivery room in my case
but that there is no need to use the
delivery table.

Dr. K. says that the hospital requires   Dr. A. says that since the hospital
NPO.   requires NPO, he suggests that I stay
home until labor is well advanced.

Dr. K. says that it is unreasonable   Dr. A. says that it is unreasonable
for a woman to expect to be in con-   for attendants to expect to control
trol in labor.   labor.

Dr. K. is disparaging of studies done   Dr. A. says that foreign studies pro-
outside the United States.   vide a different and often refreshing
perspective.

Dr. K. says that if I eat too much,   Dr. A. says good nutrition, contain-
the baby will be too large for a vag-   ing protein, carbohydrates, and
inal delivery and that his vitamin   essential fatty acids, as well as vita-

111

Bad Signs	*Good Signs*
prescription is enough to ensure adequate fetal development.	mins and minerals, is necessary to grow a strong baby, placenta, and uterus.
Dr. K. is always rushed and trying to cut the visit short.	Dr. A. always waits for me to signal the end of the visit.
Dr. K. asks why I want what I want in a hostile tone that makes me feel that I have no right to want anything, or in an incredulous tone that makes me feel that he has grave reservations about my sanity.	Dr. A. asks why I want what I want in an interested tone that makes me feel that he wants to understand what I am after.
Dr. K. says that women make too big a deal out of birth and that they should just get done with it and go home.	Dr. A. says that he never knew a woman who wanted to forget a good birth experience or was able to forget a bad one.
When my friend's baby was born, Dr. K. said, "Well, we finally made a woman of you."	When my friend's baby was born, Dr. A. said, "Congratulations! You did a beautiful job."
Dr. K. told me, "If you're not going to let me do anything, why should I be your doctor?"	Dr. A. says, "The less you need me, the better."
Dr. K. said, "Your pelvis seems a little narrow. I think that you may need a cesarean."	Dr. A. said, "I've seen women with narrow pelves like yours get their babies down. But, in any case, it's a good idea to practice squatting."
Dr. K. says a private labor assistant is unnecessary and will get in the way.	Dr. A. says that he encourages his patients to bring in their own labor assistant because the patients might

Bad Signs	*Good Signs*
	not be as comfortable with hospital staff, especially if the unit is very busy.
Dr. K. is always telling me about the babies he has rescued from asphyxiation.	Dr. A. told me that his favorite birth was one in which the mother pushed his hand away and removed the loop of cord that was around her baby's neck herself.
Dr. K. says I'll have to have an IV to avoid getting dehydrated.	Dr. A. says I should try to sip clear fluids frequently during labor, to prevent dehydration and the need for IV fluids.
Dr. K. offered my friend forceps when she was having trouble pushing her baby down.	Dr. A. helped my friend squat on the floor when she was having trouble getting her baby down.
Dr. K. says an episiotomy is better than a tear.	Dr. A. says that when forceps are not used, the dorsal position is avoided, and pushing is not overdone, tears are minimal and do not justify episiotomy.
Dr. K. says he likes to rupture the membranes during active labor to check the amniotic fluid for meconium (fecal staining due to relaxation of the fetus's anal sphincter, as may occur in fetal distress).	Dr. A. says that if he thinks it would be helpful to check for meconium, he will look through the membranes with an amnioscope.
Dr. K. says that if he thinks a woman is likely to need a cesarean, he sees no point in putting her through the pain of labor.	Dr. A. says that he is impressed that many of his patients are glad to have experienced labor, even when they needed a cesarean in the end.

11

A PREGNANT PAUSE

ONCE you have chosen your care providers, you can relax and enjoy pregnancy. It is a very special state of being that is experienced all too fleetingly in our culture of small families. It is also an ideal time to get used to trusting your body's messages. When you are hungry, it is time to eat. But don't defeat the system with highly processed foods that have all the flavors that your body is asking for with none of the nutrients it expects to get at the same time. Also keep in mind that frequent small meals decrease nausea and heartburn, fiber (in fruits and vegetables and in whole grains) reduces constipation, and calcium (in milk products) helps prevent muscle cramps.

Body messages also provide guidance for physical activity. When you are tired, you should take a rest, and when you are restless, you should treat yourself to a brisk walk or some other comfortable exercise. Remember that when you are out of breath, your baby is too, and adjust the pace of your activity accordingly. If your back starts to hurt, do gentle exercises that will gradually strengthen it and wear comfortable shoes. Using a maternity girdle instead will make your back still weaker and less prepared to carry your baby around after it is born. In general, continue all activities that you enjoy, including sex, in whatever form and to whatever degree you find comfortable. Unless the doctor has specific reasons to think that the pregnancy is less stable than normal, the uterine contractions induced at orgasm should have no adverse effects. Indeed, they may actually have beneficial effects, if only in creating positive associations in your mind preparatory to labor. It is also worth-while to maintain physical avenues of communication with your mate because these can help ease pain and promote progress in labor.

During the course of your pregnancy, your doctor (or midwife) will be seeing you regularly to check how you are doing. The purpose of these prenatal visits is to prevent problems and to detect any that do occur early enough to minimize their consequences. As emphasized earlier, the best prevention is a healthy life style. A good doctor will remind you of this during office visits. However, preexisting conditions (physiological, anatomical, infectious, or genetic) may prejudice the course of your pregnancy. A thorough history and examination in the first prenatal visit is intended to identify any potential problems. The physical examination will reveal any anatomical abnormalities. Blood pressure, heart rate, urine protein, and urine sugar provide measures of the condition of physiological control systems. Blood tests check for anemia, infection, immunity to rubella, Rh incompatibility, and irregular antibodies. Cultures of urine and vaginal mucus detect infections of the pelvic area. A thorough history will note previous problems and uncover any familial tendency to genetic or other complications. This may, in turn, suggest other pertinent tests (see below).

The history will also try to establish the date of conception. This is extremely important in evaluating fetal growth during pregnancy and in identifying prematurity and postmaturity issues at the end of pregnancy. Apart from a healthy life style and a good choice of physician, the most important contribution you can make to your prenatal care is to be familiar enough with your body to know when conception took place. This means recording the dates of your periods until they stop and keeping track of variations in your sexual activity. If you have been checking your basal temperature or vaginal mucus as an indicator of fertility, this information is also useful.

The same criteria apply to care during pregnancy as apply to care during labor. Procedures that provide useful information at little or no cost or risk should be routine. An example in labor is intermittent auscultation of the fetal heart rate. In prenatal care, routine procedures, following the initial history and examination, include periodic urine analysis, blood-pressure measurement, weight determination, abdominal estimation of fetal growth, auscultation of the fetal heart rate (when it becomes audible), and assessment of any complaints the mother may have. Routine prenatal care should include *only* those procedures with little or no cost or risk. Since the risks of ultrasound exposure are not fully understood, the recent National Institutes of Health Consensus Development Conference on Ultrasound Imaging in Pregnancy recommended that it not be used routinely. Similarly, recent evidence of increased premature membrane rupture following digital examination of the cervix in late pregnancy suggests that this weekly tradition should no longer be routine.[1]

When the initial history or routine examination indicates cause for concern, special tests or therapy may be recommended. These need to be scrutinized very carefully with respect to the balance between costs and risks, on the one hand, and potential benefits, on the other. Seek a second opinion for *any* situation that puzzles or worries you. But, with or without a second opinion, you should base your assessment of the desirability of a procedure on specific information.

The first thing you need to know is exactly what the test or therapy entails and what is known or suspected about the associated *risks*. For example, any test requiring amniotic fluid involves insertion of a needle into the uterus with the guidance of an ultrasound image to prevent injuring the placenta or the baby. Risks include a possibility of miscarriage and some exposure to ultrasound. The stress test for fetal well-being in postdate pregnancies often involves a supine position and oxytocin infusion. These are the very conditions that can precipitate fetal distress in labor. Depending on the circumstances, these risks may not seem worthwhile.

The second thing you need to know about a proposed test or therapy is what *benefit* it will provide. For a test to be beneficial, the information it provides must be both accurate and influential. If the test is unreliable (i.e., frequently gives false positive or negative results), it may not be worth doing. If the results, however accurate, will not influence subsequent care substantially, the test is also not worthwhile. For example, amniocentesis to check for chromosomal abnormalities is inappropriate if the mother does not intend to abort an affected fetus and intrauterine therapy is not an option. Mother and baby should not be subjected to risks to satisfy curiosity or engage in a fishing expedition.

For a therapy to be beneficial, the problem to be addressed must be clearly and accurately identified, and the procedure to be used must have a proven record of ameliorating that problem. If the problem is incorrectly diagnosed, the therapy can have disastrous consequences. Even if the problem is correctly diagnosed, the therapy available may hurt more than it helps. Do not hesitate to ask for the relevant research data in these situations. And when in doubt, get a second opinion from a specialist.

The final step in considering a test or therapy should be an exploration of *alternatives*. One alternative, of course, is to do nothing. This is the implicit alternative against which the risks and benefits of any procedure are compared. However, there are often other alternatives. For example, toward the end of pregnancy, fetal well-being may be evaluated by a stress test, a nonstress test, or simply by counting fetal movements on a regular basis.[2] In addition, the stress test itself may be done with nipple stimulation as a substitute for intravenous oxytocin.[3] All alternatives should be subjected to the same consideration of risks and benefits as the originally proposed procedure. In the end you may decide that the original proposal was best, but you cannot lose by having first checked into alternatives.

Should a high-risk situation develop, it is important to be open to the idea of referral to a high-risk center. If your doctor doesn't suggest it, you can take the initiative. Timely referral is especially important in premature labor. If it seems likely that your baby will need intensive care, it is better to transfer to a tertiary care center in labor than to wait until the baby is born and struggling.[4]

Between your checkups, you will naturally be giving some thought to your baby's future needs. Choosing a pediatrician is usually easier than choosing an obstetrician, and the skills that you developed in the earlier search will be useful in this next one. Again, read enough to decide what kind of care you want, ask acquaintances what they like and dislike about the pediatricians they know, and select from among these a few likely prospects to interview. A good pediatrician should communicate well with parents and children, and be interested in social as well as physical well-being. With regard to perinatal issues, he should be supportive of your wishes for natural childbirth, actively interested in overcoming any barriers to breast feeding (especially for premature infants),[5] and thoughtful and informed about the controversies surrounding neonatal routines, including circumcision. He should also be open-minded about family life styles, an advocate of parents living-in with hospitalized children, an educator in matters of child safety (e.g., suitable automotive safety restraints from birth onward, protection against poisonous household chemicals and plants, selection of safe toys and foods), and knowledgeable about local day-care resources.

Circumcision is the one aspect of infant medical care that is often delegated to the obstetrician. As practiced routinely in this country, circumcision is done in the hospital before discharge (now usually within two to three days of birth). The operation takes place with the infant's arms and legs strapped to a board. The procedure may be particularly prolonged in techniques which emphasize hard clamping of the tissue to avoid bleeding. There is no analgesia or anesthesia and no comfort from parents. As our appreciation of the sensory capabilities of newborns has increased in recent years, this routine has come under greater scrutiny. At present, the general consensus is that in our society (with our climate and our standards of hygiene) no convincing evidence exists of medical advantages to routine circumcision and that circumcision can be done later in life, if needed. This turnabout in medical opinion is difficult for many parents to understand and is no help to those parents who want circumcision for reasons of social identification (religious, paternal, fraternal, or otherwise). The burden of justification for circumcision would be greatly reduced if the procedure was practiced more humanely. Traditional Judaic circumcision is not done until the child is eight days old. It is done in his own home, while held by his godfather.

The traditional technique is quick, to the point that it is often over before the child starts to protest. A drop of wine is given immediately for pain relief, and the child is then taken to his mother to be nursed to sleep. If you intend to circumcise a son, then you may want to inquire in your community about such alternatives.

Although breast feeding is practiced widely now, the drop-out rate during the first few weeks is high. If you are a first-time mother (or one who has not breast-fed before), it is worthwhile to get in touch with the local chapter of La Leche League. This self-help organization is primarily responsible for the resurgence of breast feeding in this country, which has been reinforced by the American Academy of Pediatrics' recent endorsement of human milk as the best food for babies. Monthly La Leche League meetings provide useful information, supportive interactions, and helpful contacts. The chapters also offer one-on-one help with any breast-feeding problems, over the phone or in a home visit. If La Leche League is not listed in your telephone book, the national office (see the resource list at the end of the book) can identify the chapter closest to you and provide you with copies of their literature.

If you expect to use day care regularly during the baby's first year, it is worthwhile to survey what is available before he is born. It takes some sleuthing and thought to find the best care, and anything less will not give you the peace of mind necessary to work effectively. In many areas good child care is in high demand and may require some reservation in advance. To make realistic plans, you should keep in mind that newborns do not remain newborns long. Within a few weeks they become bored with predictable mobiles and particularly enjoy watching older children play. Toward the middle of the first year, they begin to develop stranger anxiety and have greater trouble accepting care from unfamiliar people in unfamiliar places. For these reasons, it is good for the baby to start part-time day care early. Beginning early and gradually adding hours also help you to develop confidence in the care provider and make any necessary adjustments in your arrangements before you go back to work.

Day care may be obtained in free-standing centers, in providers' homes, and in your own home. Early childhood development specialists recommend family day care (care of a small group of children in the provider's home) for children under three years old. (By age three, most children are ready for a richer and more structured program of activities than individuals at home can usually provide.) Family day care for infants and toddlers has the advantage of an extended-family-like environment with a single primary care provider and a group of children of various ages to watch, imitate, and interact with. Although there are always notable exceptions, family day care tends to be more stable and reliable than home care and more personal and flexible than center care.

The fracturing of family structure and the evolution of specialized roles in our society have put us in the position of relying on strangers to care for our children when we work, to provide guidance in breast feeding, and to encourage a healthy life style in pregnancy. These support systems are no longer built in and automatic. However, when sought out and cultivated, they can be highly effective.

12

PARTING

A S your pregnancy progresses, you will be making final preparations for your baby's birth. It is helpful to have these completed and other obligations settled before your due date so that there are no unnecessary psychophysiological impediments to the timely onset of labor. If you are going to hire a labor assistant (and, as indicated in Chapter 4 and below, I urge you to do so), she should be chosen for her compatibility, experience, and reliability. In respect to the first, she should be able to communicate well with you and should sympathize with your childbirth protocol. To assess her experience and reliability, you may want to talk to mothers she has worked with previously. Other measures of her reliability are the limit she places on the number of women she agrees to attend with due dates in a given period and the arrangements she makes for being reached when she is available and for her backup when she is not. If you have previously had a cesarean delivery, she should have attended some VBACs (vaginal births after cesarean) or at least know a lot about them. If you cannot find or afford a good experienced labor assistant, consider whether one of your friends could act in that capacity. An empathetic, nurturing, well-informed, clearheaded, unflappable woman, familiar with unmedicated birth (preferably in her own birth experiences but otherwise through books like this one and films with full color and sound—see Resources), can be helpful if you explain in some detail what it is that you would like from her.

If, after all the reading you have done, you still want to take child-birth classes for reinforcement or interaction, beware of those that emphasize the smorgasbord view of obstetrical technology (especially hospital-sponsored classes) and those that have rigid, unresponsive protocols for behaving during contractions. By contacting the nearest child-birth educators' association (see the resource list at the back of the book), you can find out who in your area teaches classes with a suitable point of view. Usually the best classes for natural childbirth, in terms of useful information and positive attitude, are the home-birth classes (see Chapter 8).

If you have children who will be present during the baby's birth, you also need to make arrangements for their preparation and supervision. With respect to the latter, keep in mind that a child's reaction to a situation is strongly influenced by the attitude of the adults around him. It is important, therefore, that the children be supervised by someone with a positive view of those aspects of birth that some might find disturbing (e.g., the appearance and sounds of extreme effort, exposure of the genitals, general nakedness, blood, and the placenta). Since you personally will not be able to provide comfort or explanation to the children during the birth, you should make a point of going with them to see realistic childbirth films (see Resources), using that opportunity to anticipate, explain, and reassure. In addition, anatomical models and birthing dolls (see the resource list at the back of the book for examples) can be very effective in helping children understand where the baby is growing and how it will get out. You may also enjoy sharing some photographs and drawings of fetal development and birth with your youngsters (again, see the resource list for examples). Children often find these fascinating and ask to see them again and again, both before and after the birth, with new comments and questions from time to time. Finally, it is important to be sure that the children understand that if you need special help (i.e., surgery), they will not be able to go with you. Their supervisor should understand that if the children become uncomfortable, hungry, bored, or tired, she is expected to attend to their needs elsewhere.

Once you have your human support system organized, you should give a little thought to physical support. It is a good idea to stock up on labor foods in advance, so you know they'll be there when you want them. You may also want to obtain a small birthing stool to take with you to the hospital. The commercially available stools are attractive but expensive. If your labor assistant doesn't have one you can use, a crude but effective stool can be constructed by sawing away the front of a wooden toilet seat and mounting the remaining seat on blocks of wood at the height most comfortable for you. A tension bar (sold for chinning exercises) can also be useful for supporting an upright birth position. If the labor room has its own lavatory, the tension bar can be placed in the doorway at the height most convenient for you. On the chance that you may want to spend some time in bed, it's a good idea to have a couple of pillows of your own to supplement the hospital supply. A thin, soft, plastic cover (e.g., a dry cleaner's bag) between the pillow and the case will protect the pillow without creating an unpleasant sensation. Any other comforts that you expect will be useful should also be made ready, and several extra copies of your protocol should be prepared to take along.

Critical among your preparations is the cultivation of a positive mindset that will help you in labor. Nancy Wainer Cohen suggests devising a list of affirmations that you repeat until you believe them in your heart as well as your head. She includes, ''I will accept my labor and believe that it is the right labor for me and my baby,'' ''Contractions assist my baby into the world,'' and ''I am strong, confident, assured, assertive and still feminine.'' I would also suggest, ''I have the final responsibility for judging what is right for me and my baby,'' ''I am attentive to my body's messages and respond to them, without worrying what people around me think of my behavior,'' and ''I will concentrate on my labor and not let the unexpected rattle me.'' If you have trouble saying these things with conviction, then you have some extra work to do. If there are emotional, social, or philosophical barriers to letting go (i.e., cooperating with your body) in labor, it is best to discover these in advance so that you can try to resolve them.

Hopefully, you now have a good working relationship with your obstetrician. If you have found one who sympathizes with your preferences and values your participation in decision making, then mutual trust and a comfortable dialogue should develop naturally and stand you in good stead during birth. However, this ideal situation may be unavailable (e.g., due to financial or geographic constraints) or may fall through at the last moment (e.g., if the doctor is unexpectedly detained when you are in labor). Thus, it is important to develop a laid-back strategy for handling any potential conflict that may arise. Tension in labor is bad for you and your baby. You should not try, and others should not ask you, to engage in debate during labor. To minimize diversion of your energy from your labor, you should have a repertoire of two- or three-syllable phrases (such as those listed at the end of this chapter) ready for you to communicate directly with attendants and for you to cue your mate and your assistant.

The most common need is to buy time either to consider or to avoid intervention. If an attendant asks whether you want X or Y, the simplest thing to say is "Maybe later." If he tells you that *he* wants you to have X or Y, you can simply say, "Not now." If he asks why, you can simply say, "Because." If he asks when, you can simply say, "We'll see." If he says that that's not good enough or that he can't go along with it, then you can firmly but sincerely say, "I'm sorry," knowing that he cannot legally abandon you without securing an agreeable substitute. You should *never* let yourself be railroaded into making a decision you might later regret. You are well within your rights to make your own choices for your own reasons. You should not try to justify your decisions unless you feel up to it. You should not be put on the defensive or be drawn into an argument. The burden is on the care provider to give a convincing justification for any procedure. If he continues to pester, you can ignore him, say "Shhh," ask him to "be quiet," or tell him to "go away." By this point, your mate or assistant should be quietly intervening on your behalf, explaining your need for time in more elaborate terms and securing peace and privacy.

Except in an emergency, which is rare in unmedicated births, your mate and your labor assistant should see to it that you take as much private time as you want (but no less than three contractions worth) to consider alternatives. Except in an emergency, doing nothing, going for a walk, changing position, and changing atmosphere are *always* alternatives to medical intervention and should *always* be considered. Time alone is *never* an indication for intervention. An extra advantage of having a labor assistant is that it allows your mate to go to the bathroom, take a rest, or get some food without leaving you to cope alone. Although you have the legal right to refuse intervention, it is difficult to exercise that right during the consuming stages of labor unless your mate and your labor assistant are there to encourage your efforts, on the one hand, and to help you make your wishes clear, on the other. When both are present, one can concentrate on communicating with attendants while the other concentrates on your needs.

Other tried and true ways can be used to buy time. The most important one is eating well in early labor, which forestalls exhaustion and the need for medical delivery, and may also reduce pain and the need for medications. Frequent, small amounts of food are generally most comfortable, but you should follow your appetite. Except when you are napping, you should not allow yourself to forget about nourishment. To be sensible, however, choose easily digested foods (i.e., low in fat and low in particulate residue and roughage). These will clear your system quickest, giving your body more immediate benefit, leaving your stomach less heavy, and minimizing the danger of pulmonary aspiration syndrome, should anesthesia become necessary. Good labor foods include clear juices (e.g., apple, cranberry), clear broth (preferably homemade with little salt), sweetened tea, plain crackers and toast (with no seeds), and strained fruits (e.g., applesauce and mashed bananas).

Another way of buying time is to stay home until active labor has started. The latent phase of labor is the longest and the most susceptible to environmental inhibition. It is exhausting and discouraging to go to the hospital only to be sent home again. It is also bad to be stuck in the hospital with a slow labor while your doctor watches the clock, the nurses change shifts, the anesthesiologists keep you from eating, and you begin to wonder if your body can do its job. If this is your first baby and you don't feel confident about your ability to judge how long to stay home, ask your labor assistant to be with you at home in early labor. Her help on the way to the hospital will also be welcome.

Once you are admitted to the hospital, another way to buy time is to minimize exams. Unless you desperately need evidence of progress to keep you going, you should meet the contractions one at a time and not make your attendants any more aware than they already are of how long you've been working. If they ask for an exam, you should ask "Why?" and "What difference will the results make?" Remember that all hospital patients have the right to refuse to be examined by anyone at any time. If your membranes have already ruptured, exams increase the risk of infection and the need to hurry the delivery. If the membranes are intact, examination carries a small risk of accidental rupture and a large temptation for intentional rupture. As discussed in Chapter 3, artificial rupture of membranes sometimes causes an abrupt change in the character of the labor, a change that is hard to cope with. In addition, it increases the pressure on the baby's head and increases the risk of infection. If it is necessary to stimulate the labor, membrane rupture is preferable to drugs, but such stimulation is seldom necessary. In general, walking, a warm shower or bath, and physical attentions from your mate are the best ways to improve the effectiveness of labor.

When you are being examined or when you are concentrating on a contraction, it is difficult to keep track of what is going on around you. Indeed, in order to be really comfortable you should not even feel it necessary to pay attention to the activities of others. Therefore, it is imperative that your mate or your assistant do it for you. While one is concentrating on helping you, the other should be prepared to ask attendants to stop and explain anything that they are doing or using. During exams and delivery someone should watch carefully what the nurse picks up or lays out because it will be in the doctor's hands next. Many women have had the hooks for rupturing membranes, the spiral scalp electrodes for fetal monitoring, and the scissors for episiotomy used before they were even aware that such procedures were contemplated. If an IV is running, your mate or assistant should read and discuss its contents with you and the contents should be rechecked if the bag is changed. If someone starts to introduce a syringe (for pain medication) or infusion pump (for oxytocin) into the IV, he should be asked to stop, to explain, and to wait for consent. Once an infusion pump is attached, any change in the settings (particularly the pump rate) should be explained beforehand and agreed to. If oxytocin is being infused, your mate or assistant will need to watch that the contractions stay far enough apart while the other gives you the extra support you will need. You should not hesitate to insist that the infusion be turned down or stopped if contractions become too long or closely spaced.

Indeed, you should not be reluctant to withdraw any previous consent you've given. Monitors can be detached (although they generally shouldn't be if drugs are in use), IVs can be removed or closed (with a heparin lock to prevent blood clotting), anesthesia can be allowed to wear off, and permission for surgery can be revoked at any time before the first cut. If time has elapsed between the decision for a cesarean delivery and the completion of preparations, you can ask for another exam to see if there has been unexpected progress. Surgery has occasionally been avoided this way. Similarly, if you give permission for anesthesia, ask for one more exam *just before* it is administered. Each strong contraction can produce significant progress, and you may find that you are closer to full dilation than you realized. You don't want to be among the women who find themselves freshly anesthetized just when it comes time to push the baby down.

As far as pushing is concerned, it is best, as usual, to do what seems comfortable. Often the maternity-unit staff will urge you to push as soon as dilation is complete, even if you do not feel ready to (i.e., your uterus has not yet converted fully to second-stage contractions). If this happens, you can tell them, "When I'm ready." If they persist in cheerleading, you should ask for "quiet." Unless the baby's condition calls for rapid delivery, you should not exhaust yourself or your baby by pushing sooner or harder than feels right. At the other extreme, some women who have felt a strong urge to push have been told that they couldn't possibly be fully dilated and that they'd better not push, until the sight of the baby's crowning head suddenly convinced the disbelievers. If you feel a distinct urge to push, then by all means insist (with the help of your assistant or mate) on examination to verify full dilation. You should not have to resist pushing unnecessarily, but you also don't want to risk irritating the cervix by pushing too soon. It should go without saying that the baby's birth should never be delayed for the benefit of a tardy doctor. In the past, such shenanigans caused cerebral palsy and worse. If the baby comes sooner than expected, he will have to be caught by whoever is closest. It is not unusual for a doctor to miss a fast birth, and such births are usually so simple that it doesn't matter.

In the final stages of birth remember that you are in charge. If you are afraid you will be whisked to the delivery room at the last minute, then stay off the bed (or anything else with wheels). If you do land in the delivery room, for whatever reason, remember that you don't have to get on the delivery table. If you do find yourself on the delivery table, remember that you can roll over to a side-lying position. You can also get back off the table. If you don't trust the doctor to take good care of your perineum, then keep it close to the floor (or the sheets, if you are in bed) and breathe your baby out gently. Your labor assistant and mate should help you squat and remind you to go slowly when the perineum is bulging. When the baby's head is born, you can lean back to check for a nuchal cord (looped around the baby's neck). Then lean forward again to facilitate birth of the baby's shoulders. All this can be done in an easygoing, low-keyed manner. Hopefully, the doctor and nurse will appreciate what you are doing. But, while giving birth, you can be legitimately oblivious to whatever shock waves may be rippling around you.

PARTING

A MOTHER'S LABOR AND DELIVERY REPERTOIRE

" (silence) "	Anytime you're not ready to talk
"Why?" "What for?" "Maybe later," "Not now" "We'll see"	Proposed Intervention and Exams
"Stop," "Wait" "Slow," "Careful"	Intervention and Exams
"Shhh," "Quiet" "Go away," "Stop it"	Interference
"Out," "Rails down" "No belts," "No wires"	Confinement
"Because" "I just do" "I just don't"	Justification
"Help" "I'm hot," "I'm cold" "Up," "Down," "Over" "Press," "Rub" "Juice," "Pillows" "Stool," "Commode"	Support
"I need to . . .," "I am going to . . ." (push, walk, etc.)	Anytime
"May I . . .," "Can I . . ."	Never

13

GETTING IT BACK TOGETHER

THE extensive denial that characterizes our culture's attitude toward birth also extends into the postpartum period. The baby that you have lived with for the last nine months has suddenly become the new sweetheart of the rest of the world. They greet his arrival with delight, while you adjust to his departure. Hopefully, this adjustment is a smooth one. However, if your bottom is sorer than you think it should be, or you are more tired than you expected to be, or you are trying to understand why you had a forceps or cesarean delivery, you may resent the uncomprehending euphoria of the world around you and its efforts not to notice that you are having trouble sitting up or sitting down, as the case may be. It is not a good idea to try to suppress any concerns or misgivings that you may have. Although there is no need to wallow in them, there is also no point in pretending they aren't there or insisting they shouldn't be. Your feelings are real and will resolve most rapidly when recognized and accepted as legitimate. They do *not* mean that you are ungrateful for or unhappy with your baby. Nor do they mean that you are ungrateful for or unhappy with the family and friends who are so eager to welcome him. This is not an either-or situation. You may be elated about your new relationship with your baby and thrilled to introduce him to the world, while being puzzled at or disappointed in some aspect of his birth. Although everyone is happy to share the former with you, many people find it hard to share the latter. Indeed, it is a rare obstetrician who understands the concerns and disappointment of a cesarean mother well enough and is comfortable enough with the emotions involved to be able to offer even as much sympathy as "I know this has been hard on you, and I wish it hadn't been necessary."

It is important, then, that, at the very least, you be kind to yourself. Every birth has its own wrinkles, and it is unfair to blame yourself if things did not go exactly as you had hoped or expected. You should realize that whatever glitches occurred in spite of all your efforts, there would have been many, many more without your efforts. Even if you didn't get everything you wanted, you've made it easier for yourself and others to get it next time. You can congratulate yourself for doing as well as you did.

As always, it helps to pay attention to what your body is telling you. The natural opiates that were produced for the birth are disappearing, and the enhanced estrogen level that generated that special sense of well-being in pregnancy is plummeting to the pseudomenopausal level that will obtain during lactation. While your uterus is continuing to contract, your metabolic machinery is working hard to shed the extra fluid and tissue mass remaining from the pregnancy and also to start up milk production. With typical wishful thinking, our culture has developed the myth that primitive women resume their usual work immediately following childbirth. But the fact is that in all known societies, past and present, women are expected to rest for an extended period after giving birth.[1] So give yourself a break, and rest with your baby whenever you can. As you marvel at the wonderful creature you produced, appreciate also the tremendous work that your body continues to do in completing the job.

If you feel unwell, don't hesitate to get help. Extended perineal discomfort may be due to a sloppily stitched episiotomy or tear and may be relieved by more expert repair. A poorly healing cesarean incision should also be attended to, as should a fever. An infectious-disease specialist should be consulted for any fever that does not respond promptly to antibiotic therapy. Persistent pelvic infection can cause long-term problems, including infertility.

After several weeks you should make a point of getting a copy of your hospital record for your files. If you still have any unresolved concerns about what went on during your baby's birth, you may find the answers you are looking for there. If not, you should review the record with your obstetrician at your postpartum checkup. In addition, you should make an effort to communicate in writing with all your obstetrical care providers, including, if appropriate, the hospital's chief of obstetrics and the head nurse of the labor and delivery unit. To the extent that you were happy with their care, your thanks will give them well-earned encouragement. To the extent that you were unhappy with their care, your feedback can help them to improve. The more specific your letter is as to what you did or didn't like and why, the more useful it is to the care providers and the more beneficial it is to women following you with similar preferences. However, keep in mind that people don't like to hear that they've failed you. If you feel that they have, a friendly, constructive tone will help get past defenses. Harsh language is best reserved for those individuals whose behavior was so out of bounds that they can be assumed to be incapable of understanding anything subtle.

Whatever your childbirth experience has been, you will certainly have learned a lot about yourself and about our medical-care system. If nothing else, I hope that you come away with the confidence as a consumer that will help you get the best from the system in your future needs. In this respect, the benefit to your baby, yourself, and the rest of your family goes way beyond whatever you were able to achieve in this birth.

RESOURCES

The following is a list of resources that I consider especially useful in one respect or another. Each will, in turn, lead you to others according to your interests.

LIBRARIES

Many of the books listed below should be in your public library. If not, you would be doing your community a favor by suggesting that the library expand its collection in this area. In the meantime, your library may be able to get the material for you through an interlibrary loan.

I also urge you to visit your nearest medical school or teaching-hospital library, if possible. Access to these libraries is often granted to the public on a courtesy basis or for a nominal fee (without borrowing privileges). If the access is limited to a few days per year, you should budget part of the time for early browsing and save the other days for later, when you may be looking for specific information. When you arrive, ask the reference librarian to describe the layout of the library—specifically the location of the research journals, the monographs, and the copying machines. For simple browsing, you should leaf through the current issues of some of the well-respected journals cited in the notes. It is not vital that you understand everything that you read, although you will find it easier than you might imagine. What is useful is to become aware of the range of issues that obstetricians debate among themselves and the manner in which that discourse takes place.

The journals contain several types of articles. The most useful are the reviews and the research reports. Review articles give a summary of the status of a particular problem as elucidated over the years by various investigators. Research articles report the results of a specific new study by one group of investigators. A research article is usually prefaced by an abstract briefly describing the purpose of the research, the procedures, the results, and the conclusions. The beginning of the article itself usually gives some background describing the status of the problem in question and the motivation for the new contribution. The end of the article discusses the new results and their implications. The material in between provides the technical details that allow the reader to evaluate critically the credibility of the data and the validity of the conclusions. Which parts of an article you read will depend upon your interest.

If you need help with the jargon, you can ask the reference librarian for a medical dictionary. If particular topics are of concern to you, you may find the *Index Medicus* and the *Science Citation Index* useful for tracking down relevant articles. The reference librarian can show you where these volumes are kept and which pages give the instructions for use. While you are in the reference section, you might have a look at the *Who's Who Directory of Medical Specialists*. This publication lists all the physicians who are board-certified in obstetrics and gynecology in your area and describes their training and hospital appointments. Also in the reference section are the *Physicians' Desk Reference* (or *PDR*), which gives manufacturers' indications, contraindications, and known side effects for all prescription drugs (e.g., oxytocin, anesthetics, prenatal vitamins) and the *AMA Drug Evaluations,* which provides independent information on commonly prescribed or administered drugs.

INFORMATION ON PREGNANCY, BIRTH AND THE NEWBORN

Birth Reborn, Michel Odent (New York: Pantheon, 1984).

Caring for Your Unborn Child, Ronald E. Gots and Barbara A. Gots (Briarcliff Manor, N.Y.: Stein & Day, 1977).

Childbirth with Love, Niels H. Lauersen (New York: Putnam's Sons, 1983).

Commonsense Childbirth, Lester Dessez Hazell (New York: Berkeley, 1984).

The Complete Book of Pregnancy and Childbirth, Sheila Kitzinger (New York: Knopf, 1982).

The Family Bed: An Age Old Concept in Childrearing, Tine Thevenin (Minneapolis: self-published,* 1976).

A Good Birth, a Safe Birth, Diane Korte and Roberta Scaer (Toronto: Bantam, 1984).

Home Oriented Maternity Experience—a Comprehensive Guide to Home Birth, H.O.M.E., Inc. (Washington, D.C.: self-published,* 1976).

Immaculate Deception, Suzanne Arms (South Hadley, Mass.: Bergin & Garvey, 1984).

The Pregnancy after 30 Workbook, ed. Gail Sforza Brewer (Emmaus, Pa.: Rodale, 1978).

Silent Knife: Cesarean Prevention and Vaginal Birth after Cesarean, Nancy Wainer Cohen and Lois J. Estner (South Hadley, Mass.: Bergin & Garvey, 1983).

Unnecessary Cesareans: Ways to Avoid Them, Diony Young and Charles Mahan (Minneapolis: ICEA,* 1980).

---

*These and many other books may be ordered from the International Childbirth Education Association Bookcenter, P.O. Box 20048, Minneapolis, Minnesota 55420.

The Womanly Art of Breastfeeding, La Leche League, International (Franklin Park, Ill.: self-published,* 1981).

PERSONAL ACCOUNTS OF PREGNANCY AND BIRTH

Birth Stories—The Experience Remembered, ed. Janet I. Ashford (Trumansburg, N.Y.: Crossing Press, 1984).

Ever since Eve—Personal Reflections on Childbirth, Nancy Caldwell Sorel (New York: Oxford, 1984).

Labor among Primitive Peoples, George J. Englemann (St. Louis: Chambers, 1883).

Labor and Delivery—an Observer's Diary, Constance A. Bean (Garden City, N.Y.: Doubleday, 1977).

Spiritual Midwifery, Ina May Gaskin (Summertown, Tenn.: The Book Publishing Co., 1977).

A Woman in Residence, Michelle Harrison (New York: Random House, 1982).

BIRTH FILMS

Birth in the Squatting Position, Polymorph Films, 118 South Street, Boston, Massachusetts 02111. (Reviewed in *Birth and the Family Journal* 6 [1979]: 29.)

Birth Place, Methodist Hospital, Film Project Coordinator, 309 West Washington Avenue, Madison, Wisconsin 53703. (Reviewed in *Birth and the Family Journal* 7 [1980]: 277.)

Common Problems in Labor and Delivery (a Breech Birth and a Shoulder Dystocia), Video Farm Productions, 156 Drake's Lane, Summertown, Tennessee 38483. (Reviewed in *Birth* 9 [1982]: 61.)

Labors of Love, Polymorph Films, 118 South Street, Boston, Massachusetts 02111.

Midwife, Cinema Medica, 2335 West Foster Avenue, Chicago, Illinois 60625. (Reviewed in *Birth and the Family Journal* 6 [1979]: 29.)

Saturday's Children, Parenting Pictures, 121 Northwest Crystal Street, Crystal River, Florida 32629. (Reviewed in *Birth* 10 [1983]: 210.)

SHARING PREGNANCY AND BIRTH WITH CHILDREN

Natalie and Bertha Rags, Monkey Business, Box 20001, Tallahassee, Florida 32304. Birthing human and monkey rag dolls.

The Visible Woman, Revell. A plastic anatomical model convertible to and from a pregnant state. Available in toy stores.

A Child Is Born: The Drama of Life before Birth, Lennart Nilsson (New York: Delacorte, 1977). A photographic essay on fetal development.

Mom and Dad and I Are Having a Baby, Maryann P. Malecki (Seattle: Pennypress, 1979). A picture book about birth for children who will be present at birth.

Children at Birth, Cinema Medica, 2335 West Foster Avenue, Chicago Illinois 60625. A color film for children in which children are present at their siblings' hospital and home births.

Birth—through Children's Eyes, Sandra VanDam Anderson and Penny Simkin (Seattle: Pennypress, 1981). A discussion for adults of the participation of children at birth.

The Flight of the Stork, Anne Bernstein (New York: Delacorte, 1978). A description for adults of the different ways children of different ages understand human reproduction.

ORGANIZATIONS

American College of Home Obstetrics
P.O. Box 25
River Forest, Illinois 60305

American College of Nurse-Midwifery
15 K Street, NW
Suite 1120
Washington, D.C. 20005

Cesarean Prevention Movement
P.O. Box 152
Syracuse, New York 13210

Cesarean / Support, Education and Concern
22 Forest Road
Framingham, Massachusetts 01701

Children in Hospitals
P.O. Box 1900
New York, New York 10001

Home Oriented Maternity Experience
511 New York Avenue,
Takoma Park, Maryland 20912

International Childbirth Education Association
P.O. Box 20048
Minneapolis, Minnesota 55420

La Leche League, International
9616 Minneapolis Avenue
Franklin Park, Illinois 60131

National Association of Parents and Professionals for Safe Alternatives
in Childbirth
P.O. Box 267
Marble Hill, Missouri 63764

NOTES

1. CHOICE

1. Margaret Hennig and Anne Jardin, *The Managerial Woman* (New York: Pocket Books, 1978).
2. A. C. Turnbull, "Introduction," in *Benefits and Hazards of the New Obstetrics,* ed. Tim Chard and Martin Richards (Philadelphia: Lippincott, 1977), pp. vi–x.

2. FORM AND FUNCTION

1. David Banta and Stephen B. Thacker, "The Risks and Benefits of Episiotomy: A Review," *Birth* 9 (1982): 25–30.
2. The fetus's role in initiating labor is well characterized in sheep. In humans it is inferred from the fact that the longest pregnancies on record have been those associated with anencephalic infants (infants with no brain or spinal cord).
3. Ernest W. Page, Claude A. Villee, and Dorothy Villee, *Human Reproduction: Essentials of Reproductive and Perinatal Medicine* (Philadelphia: Saunders, 1981), figure 15-1.
4. Susan M. Sellers, Helena T. Hodgson, Lesley M. Mountford, M. D. Mitchell, Anne B. M. Anderson, and A. C. Turnbull, "Is Oxytocin Involved in Parturition?" *British Journal of Obstetrics and Gynaecology* 88 (1981): 725–729.

   Anna-Riita Fuchs, Peter Husslein, and Fritz Fuchs, "Oxytocin and the Initiation of Human Parturition. II: Stimulation of Prostaglandin Production in Human Decidua by Oxytocin," *American Journal of Obstetrics and Gynecology* 141 (1981): 694–697.
5. Jay S. Rosenblatt, "Progress in the Study of Maternal Behavior in Ani-

mals," in *Birth, Interaction and Attachment*, ed. Marshall H. Klaus and Martha Oschrin Robertson (Skillman, N.J.: Johnson & Johnson, 1982), pp. 9–18.

6. Joseph W. Pilkington, Charles B. Nemeroff, George A. Mason, and Arthur J. Prange, Jr., "Increase in Plasma β-Endorphin-like Immunoreactivity at Parturition in Normal Women," *American Journal of Obstetrics and Gynecology* 145 (1983): 111–112 and references therein.

7. A. R. Gintzler, "Endorphin-mediated Increases in Pain Threshold during Pregnancy," *Science* 210 (1980): 193–195.

8. Robert S. Bridges and Cordelia T. Grimm, "Reversal of Morphine Disruption of Maternal Behavior by Concurrent Treatment with the Opiate Antagonist Naloxone," *Science* 218 (1982): 166–168.

9. Martin H. Johnson and Barry J. Everitt, *Essential Reproduction* (Oxford: Blackwell, 1980), p. 309.

10. Bertold Salzmann, "Rupture of Low-Segment Cesarean Section Scars," *Obstetrics and Gynecology* 23 (1964): 460–466.

11. C. Mendez-Bauer, J. Arroyo, C. Garcia-Ramos, A. Menendez, M. Lavilla, F. Izquierdo, I. Villa Elizaga, and J. Zamarriego, "Effects of Standing Position on Spontaneous Uterine Contractility and Other Aspects of Labor," *Journal of Perinatal Medicine* 3 (1975): 89–100.

A. G. Diaz, R. Schwarcz, R. Fescina, and R. Caldeyro-Barcia, "Vertical Position during the First Stage of the Course of Labor, and Neonatal Outcome," *European Journal of Obstetrics, Gynecology and Reproductive Biology* 11 (1980): 1–7.

A. M. Flynn, J. Kelly, G. Hollins, and P. F. Lynch, "The Effect of Ambulation in Labour on Uterine Action, Analgesia and Fetal Wellbeing," in *Gynecology and Obstetrics,* ed. Shoichi Sakamoto, Shimpei Tojo, and Tetsuya Nakayama (Amsterdam: Excerpta Medica, 1980), pp. 981–983.

J. Arroyos Frades, C. Mendez-Bauer, A. Menendez, L. Reina, C. Garcia-Ramos, F. Izquierdo, and J. Zamarriego, "Influence of Maternal Position during Labor on Uterine Contractility and Its Effects on Cervical Dilatation," *ibid.*, pp. 969–971.

12. J. Bieniarz, J. J. Crottogini, G. Romero-Salinas, T. Yoshida, J. J. Poseiro, and R. Caldeyro-Barcia, "Aortocaval Compression by the Uterus in Late Human Pregnancy," *American Journal of Obstetrics and Gynecology* 100 (1968): 203–217.

Kent Ueland and John M. Hansen, "Maternal Cardiovascular Dynamics. II: Posture and Uterine Contractions," *American Journal of Obstetrics and Gynecology* 103 (1969): 1–7.

13. Page *et al.*, *op. cit.*, figure 2-8.
14. R. Caldeyro-Barcia, "The Influence of Maternal Bearing-Down Efforts during Second Stage on Fetal Well-Being," *Birth and the Family Journal* 6 (1979): 19–23.
15. Betsy Lozoff, "Birth in Non-Industrial Societies," in *Birth, Interaction and Attachment,* ed. Marshall H. Klaus and Martha Oschrin Robertson (Skillman, N.J.: Johnson & Johnson, 1982), pp. 1–6.
16. Q. B. DeMarsh, H. L. Alt, and W. F. Windle, with D. S. Hillis, "The Effect of Depriving the Infant of Its Placental Blood," *Journal of the American Medical Association* 116 (1941): 2568–2573.
17. S. Kitzinger, *The Complete Book of Pregnancy and Childbirth* (New York: Knopf, 1982), p. 251.
18. Emanuel A. Friedman, "Patterns of Labor as Indicators of Risk," *Clinical Obstetrics and Gynecology* 16 (1973): 172–183.
19. Kenneth R. Niswander and Myron Gordon, *The Women and Their Pregnancies: The Collaborative Perinatal Study of the National Institutes of Neurological Diseases and Stroke* (Philadelphia: Saunders, 1972).

    R. Caldeyro-Barcia, transcribed remarks, in *Birth and the Family Journal* 2 (1975): pp. 6–7.

    W. R. Cohen, "Influence of the Duration of Second Stage Labor on Perinatal Outcome and Puerperal Morbidity," *Obstetrics and Gynecology* 49 (1977): 266–269.
20. I. R. Lange, C. Collister, J. Johnson, Dennis Cote, M. Torchia, G. Freund, and F. A. Manning, "The Effect of Vaginal Prostaglandin E-2 Pessaries on Induction of Labor," *American Journal of Obstetrics and Gynecology* 148 (1984): 621.
21. T. Chard and G. L. D. Gibbens, "Spurt Release of Oxytocin during Surgical Induction of Labor in Women," *American Journal of Obstetrics and Gynecology* 147 (1983): 678–680.
22. C. F. Goodfellow, M. G. R. Hull, D. F. Swaab, J. Dogterom, and R. M. Buijs, "Oxytocin Deficiency at Delivery with Epidural Analgesia," *British Journal of Obstetrics and Gynaecology* 90 (1983): 214–219.
23. R. R. Lenke and J. M. Nemes, "Use of Nipple Stimulation to Obtain Contraction Stress Test," *Obstetrics and Gynecology* 63 (1984): 345–348.

    J. F. Huddleston, G. Sutliff, and D. Robinson, "Contraction Stress Test by Intermittent Nipple Stimulation," *Obstetrics and Gynecology* 63 (1984): 669–673.

    E. L. Capeless and L. I. Mann, "Use of Breast Stimulation for Antepartum Stress Testing," *Obstetrics and Gynecology* 64 (1984): 641–645.

24. J. P. Elliott and J. F. Flaherty, "The Use of Breast Stimulation to Ripen the Cervix in Term Pregnancies," *American Journal of Obstetrics and Gynecology* 145 (1983): 553–556.

25. M. Phillippe, "Fetal Catecholamines," *American Journal of Obstetrics and Gynecology* 146 (1983): 840–855.

26. M. B. Strauss, "Observations on the Etiology of Toxemias of Pregnancy," *American Journal of the Medical Sciences* 190 (1935): 811–824.

27. S. E. Cloeren, T. H. Lippert, and M. Hinselmann, "Hypovolemia in Toxemia of Pregnancy: Plasma Expander Therapy with Surveillance of Central Venous Pressure," *Archiv Für Gynaekologie* 215 (1973): 123–132.

   R. Groenendijk, J. B. M. J. Trimbos, and H. C. S. Wallenberg, "Hemodynamic Measurements in Preeclampsia: Preliminary Observations," *American Journal of Obstetrics and Gynecology* 150 (1984): 232–236.

28. R. L. Naeye, "Roundtable. VI: Effects of Maternal Nutrition on Fetal and Neonatal Survival," *Birth* 10 (1983): 109–113.

29. L. Woodward, Y. Brackbill, K. McManus, P. Doering, and D. Robinson, "Exposure to Drugs with Possible Adverse Effects during Pregnancy and Birth," *Birth* 9 (1982): 165–171.

   Sarah H. Broman, "Obstetric Medications," in *Childhood Learning Disabilities and Prenatal Risk*, ed. C. C. Brown (Skillman, N.J.: Johnson & Johnson, 1983), pp. 56–64.

   Yvonne Brackbill, "Obstetrical Medication and Infant Behavior," in *Handbook of Infant Development*, ed. Joy D. Osofsky (New York: Wiley, 1979), pp. 76–125.

3. ALL OR NONE

1. Peter M. Dunn, "Obstetric Delivery Today—for Better or for Worse?" *The Lancet* (April 10, 1976): 790–793.

2. Anne M. Seiden, "The Sense of Mastery in the Childbirth Experience," in *The Woman Patient: Medical and Psychological Interfaces,* vol. 1, ed. Malkah T. Notman and Carol C. Nadelson (New York: Plenum, 1978), pp. 87–105.

   Sharron S. Humenick, "Mastery: The Key to Childbirth Satisfaction? A Review," *Birth and the Family Journal* 8 (1981): 79–83.

   Sharron S. Humenick and Larry A. Bugen, "Mastery: The Key to Childbirth Satisfaction? A Study," *Birth and the Family Journal* 8 (1981): 84–90.

3. S. G. Gabbe, B. B. Ettinger, R. K. Freeman, and C. B. Martin, "Umbilical Cord Compression Associated with Amniotomy: Laboratory Observa-

tions," *American Journal of Obstetrics and Gynecology* 126 (1976): 353–355.

M. Martell, J. M. Belizan, F. Nieto, and R. Schwarcz, "Blood Acid-Base Balance at Birth in Neonates from Labors with Early and Late Rupture of Membranes," *The Journal of Pediatrics* 89 (1976): 963–967.

F. S. Miyazaki and N. A. Taylor, "Saline Amnioinfusion for Relief of Variable or Prolonged Decelerations: A Preliminary Report," *American Journal of Obstetrics and Gynecology* 146 (1983): 670–678.

K. J. Leveno, J. G. Quirk, Jr., F. G. Cunningham, S. D. Nelson, R. Santos-Ramos, A. Toofanian, and R. T. DePalma, "Prolonged Pregnancy. I: Observations Concerning the Causes of Fetal Distress," *American Journal of Obstetrics and Gynecology* 150 (1984): 465–473.

4. J. Seitchik, J. Amico, A. G. Robinson, and M. Castillo, "Oxytocin Augmentation of Dysfunctional Labor. IV: Oxytocin Pharmacokinetics," *American Journal of Obstetrics and Gynecology* 150 (1984): 225–228.

5. R. R. Murray, "Operative Intervention in Normal Labor and Delivery," *Obstetrics and Gynecology Annual* 9 (1980): 195–212.

6. D. Banta and S. B. Thacker, "The Risks and Benefits of Episiotomy: A Review," *Birth* 9 (1982): 25–30.

7. S. Kitzinger and R. Walters, *Some Women's Experiences of Episiotomy* (London: National Childbirth Trust, 1981).

8. K. B. Nelson and S. H. Broman, "Perinatal Risk Factors in Children with Serious Motor and Mental Handicaps," *Annals of Neurology* 2 (1977): 371–377.

9. B. R. Pridmore, E. N. Hey, and W. A. Aherne, "Spinal Cord Injury of the Fetus during Delivery with Kielland's Forceps," *The Journal of Obstetrics and Gynaecology of the British Commonwealth* 81 (1974): 168–172.

10. M. G. Levine, J. Holroyde, J. R. Woods, Jr., T. A. Siddiqi, M. Scott, and M. Miodovnik, "Birth Trauma: Incidence and Predisposing Factors," *Obstetrics and Gynecology* 63 (1984): 792–795.

11. E. A. Friedman, M. R. Sachtleben-Murray, D. Dahrouge, and R. K. Neff, "Long-Term Effects of Labor and Delivery on Offspring: A Matched-Pair Analysis," *American Journal of Obstetrics and Gynecology* 150 (1984): 941–945.

12. J. D. Goldberg, W. R. Cohen, and E. A. Friedman, "Cesarean Section Indication and the Risk of Respiratory Distress Syndrome," *Obstetrics and Gynecology* 57 (1981): 30–32.

13. K. O'Driscill and M. Foley, "Correlation of Decrease in Perinatal Mortality and Increase in Cesarean Section Rates," *Obstetrics and Gynecology* 61 (1983): 1–5.

S. B. Effer, S. Saigal, C. Rand, D. J. S. Hunter, B. Stoskoph, A. C. Harper, C. Minrod, and R. Milner, "Effect of Delivery Method on Outcomes in the Very Low Birth Weight Breech Infant: Is the Improved Survival Related to Cesarean Section or Other Perinatal Care Maneuvers?" *American Journal of Obstetrics and Gynecology* 145 (1983): 123–128.

A. F. Olshan, K. K. Shy, D. A. Luthy, D. Hickok, N. S. Weiss, and J. R. Daling, "Cesarean Birth and Neonatal Mortality in Very Low Birth Weight Infants," *Obstetrics and Gynecology* 64 (1984): 267–270.

L. C. Gilstrap III, J. C. Hauth, and S. Toussaint, "Cesarean Section: Changing Incidence and Indications," *Obstetrics and Gynecology* 63 (1984): 205–208.

4. LADIES IN DISTRESS

1. L. Woodward, Y. Brackbill, K. McManus, P. Doering, and D. Robinson, "Exposure to Drugs with Possible Adverse Effects during Pregnancy and Birth," *Birth* 9 (1982): 165–171.

Sarah H. Broman, "Obstetric Medications," in *Childhood Learning Disabilities and Prenatal Risk,* ed. C. C. Brown (Skillman, N.J.: Johnson & Johnson, 1983), pp. 56–64.

Yvonne Brackbill, "Obstetrical Medication and Infant Behavior," in *Handbook of Infant Development,* ed. Joy D. Osofsky (New York: Wiley, 1979), pp. 76–125.

2. F. P. Zuspan, L. A. Cibils, and S. V. Pose, "Myometrial and Cardiovascular Responses to Alterations in Plasma Epinephrine and Norepinephrine," *American Journal of Obstetrics and Gynecology* 84 (1962): 841–851.

R. P. Lederman, E. Lederman, B. A. Work, Jr., and D. S. McCann, "The Relationship of Maternal Anxiety, Plasma Catecholamines and Plasma Cortisol to Progress in Labor," *American Journal of Obstetrics and Gynecology* 132 (1978): 495–500.

K. Adamsons, E. Mueller-Heubach, and R. E. Myers, "Production of Asphyxia in the Rhesus Monkey by Administration of Catecholamines to the Mother," *American Journal of Obstetrics and Gynecology* 109 (1971): 248–262.

R. E. Myers, "Maternal Psychological Stress and Fetal Asphyxia: A Study of the Monkey," *American Journal of Obstetrics and Gynecology* 122 (1975): 47–59.

S. M. Shnider, T. K. Abboud, R. Artal, E. H. Henriksen, S. J. Stefani, and G. Levinson, "Maternal Catecholamines Decrease during Labor after

Lumbar Epidural Anesthesia,'' *American Journal of Obstetrics and Gynecology* 147 (1983): 13–15.

3. A. M. Flynn, J. Kelly, G. Hollins, and P. F. Lynch, "The Effect of Ambulation in Labour on Uterine Action, Analgesia and Fetal Wellbeing," in *Gynecology and Obstetrics,* ed. Shoichi Sakamoto, Shimpei Tojo, and Tetsuya Nakayama (Amsterdam: Excerpta Medica, 1980) pp. 981–983.

4. Claire M. Andrews, "Changing Fetal Position," *Journal of Nurse-Midfery* 25 (1980): 7–11.

5. J. G. B. Russell, "Moulding of the Pelvic Outlet," *Journal of Obstetrics and Gynecology of the British Commonwealth* 76 (1969): 817–820.

6. Grantly Dick-Read, *Childbirth without Fear* (New York: Harper & Row, 1979).

7. David C. Glass, Bruce Reim, and Jerome E. Singer, "Behavioral Consequences of Adaptation to Controllable and Uncontrollable Noise," *Journal of Experimental Social Psychology* 7 (1971): 244–257.

8. Niles Newton, *Maternal Emotions* (New York: Hoeber, 1955).

Niles Newton and Michael Newton, "Childbirth in Crosscultural Perspective," in *Modern Perspectives in Psycho-Obstetrics,* ed. J. G. Howells (New York: Brunner / Mazel, 1972).

Niles Newton, "Interrelationships between Sexual Responsiveness, Birth and Breastfeeding," in *Contemporary Sexual Behavior: Critical Issues in the 1970s,* ed. J. Zubin and J. Money (Baltimore: The Johns Hopkins University Press, 1973), pp. 77–98.

Sheila Kitzinger, "The Woman on the Delivery Table," in *Woman on Woman,* ed. M. I. Laing (London: Sedgwick and Jackson, 1971), pp. 91–111.

9. Harold Speert, *Iconograhia Gyniatrica: A Pictoral History of Gynecology and Obstetrics* (Philadelphia: Davis, 1973), figure 4-10.

10. R. Sosa, J. Kennell, M. Klaus, S. Robertson, and J. Urrutia, "The Effect of a Supportive Companion on Perinatal Problems, Length of Labor, and Mother-Infant Interaction," *The New England Journal of Medicine* 303 (1980): 597–600.

M. Klaus, J. Kennell, and R. Sosa, "Child Health and Breastfeeding: The Effect of a Supportive Woman (Doula) during Labor and the Effect of Early Suckling," *Pediatric Research* 15 (1981): 450.

5. PRESCRIPTIONS FOR DISASTER

1. R. C. Goodlin, "On Protection of the Maternal Perineum during Birth," *Obstetrics and Gynecology* 62 (1983): 393–394.

D. Banta and S. B. Thacker, "The Risks and Benefits of Episiotomy: A Review," *Birth* 9 (1982): 25–30.

S. Kitzinger and R. Walters, *Some Women's Experiences of Episiotomy* (London: National Childbirth Trust, 1981).

2. G. S. Bause, J. R. Neibyl, and R. C. Saunders, "Doppler Ultrasound and Maternal Erythrocyte Fragility," *Obstetrics and Gynecology* 62 (1983): 7–10.

3. Roberta J. Apfel and Susan M. Fisher, *To Do No Harm, DES and the Dilemmas of Modern Medicine* (New Haven: Yale University Press, 1984).

4. F. C. Miller, K. E. Pearse, and R. H. Paul, "Fetal Heart Rate Pattern Recognition by the Method of Auscultation," *Obstetrics and Gynecology* 64 (1984): 332–336.

5. J. Lumley, "The Irresistible Rise of Electronic Fetal Monitoring," *Birth* 9 (1982): 150–151, and references contained therein.

6. R. R. Neutra, S. Greenland, and E. A. Friedman, "The Relationship between Electronic Fetal Monitoring and Apgar Score," *American Journal of Obstetrics and Gynecology* 140 (1981): 440–445.

7. *Ibid.*

8. R. A. Baker, "Technological Intervention in Obstetrics: Has the Pendulum Swung Too Far?" *Obstetrics and Gynecology* 51 (1978): 241–244.

9. Lumley, *op. cit.*

10. S. E. Cohen, "Aspiration Syndromes in Pregnancy," *The Journal of Anesthesiology* 51 (1979): 375–377, and references contained therein.

11. B. Gonik and D. B. Cotton, "Peripartum Colloid Osmotic Pressure Changes: Influence of Intravenous Hydration," *American Journal of Obstetrics and Gynecology* 150 (1984): 99–100.

12. N. B. Kenepp, W. C. Shelley, S. Kumar, B. B. Gutsche, S. Gabbe, and M. Delivoria-Papadopoulos, "Effects on Newborn of Hydration with Glucose in Patients Undergoing Cesarean Section with Regional Anesthesia," *The Lancet* (March 22, 1980): 645.

L. J. Grylack, S. S. Chu, and J. W. Scanlon, "Use of Intravenous Fluids before Cesarean Section: Effects on Perinatal Glucose, Insulin, and Sodium Homeostasis," *Obstetrics and Gynecology* 63 (1984): 654–657.

13. S. Singhi, E. Chookang, and J. St. E. Hall, "Intrapartum Infusion of Aqueous Glucose, Transplacental Hyponatraemia and Risk of Neonatal Jaundice," *British Journal of Obstetrics and Gynaecology.* 91 (1984): 1014–1018.

14. W. S. Nimmo, J. Wilson, and L. F. Prescott, "Narcotic Analgesics and Delayed Gastric Emptying during Labour," *The Lancet* (April 19, 1975): 890–893.

6. A MATTER OF TIME

1. M. L. Gimovsky, R. L. Wallace, B. S. Schifrin, and R. H. Paul, "Randomized Management of the Nonfrank Breech Presentation at Term: A Preliminary Report," *American Journal of Obstetrics and Gynecology* 146 (1983): 34–40.

J. V. Collea, C. Chein, and E. J. Quilligan, "The Randomized Management of Term Frank Breech Presentation: A Study of 208 Cases," *American Journal of Obstetrics and Gynecology* 137 (1980): 235–242.

J. E. Green, F. McLean, L. P. Smith, and R. Usher, "Has an Increased Cesarean Section Rate for Term Breech Delivery Reduced the Incidence of Birth Asphyxia, Trauma and Death?" *American Journal of Obstetrics and Gynecology* 142 (1982): 643–648.

M. G. Rosen and L. Chik, "The Effect of Delivery Route on Outcome in Breech Presentation," *American Journal of Obstetrics and Gynecology* 148 (1984): 909–914.

A. J. Jaffa, M. R. Peyser, S. Ballas, and R. Toaff, "Management of Term Breech Presentation in Primigravidae," *British Journal of Obstetrics and Gynaecology* 88 (1981): 721–724.

2. J. P. Van Dorsten, B. S. Schifrin, and R. L. Wallace, "Randomized Control Trial of External Cephalic Version with Tocolysis in Late Pregnancy," *American Journal of Obstetrics and Gynecology* 141 (1981): 417–424.

G. J. Hofmeyr, "Effect of External Cephalic Version in Late Pregnancy on Breech Presentation and Caesarean Section Rate: A Controlled Trial," *British Journal of Obstetrics and Gynaecology* 90 (1983): 392–399.

3. J. R. Harris, "Vaginal Delivery Following Cesarean Section," *American Journal of Obstetrics and Gynecology* 66 (1953): 1191–1195.

R. G. Douglas, S. J. Birnbaum, and F. A. MacDonald, "Pregnancy and Labor Following Cesarean Section," *American Journal of Obstetrics and Gynecology* 86 (1983): 961–971.

B. S. Merrill and C. E. Gibbs, "Planned Vaginal Delivery Following Cesarean Section," *Obstetrics and Gynecology* 52 (1978): 50–52.

C. J. Pauerstein, "Once a Section, Always a Trial of Labor?" *Obstetrics and Gynecology* 28 (1966): 273–276.

P. E. Lawler, M. J. Bulfin, F. C. Lawler, and P. E. Lawler, Jr., "A Review of Vaginal Delivery Following Cesarean Section from Private Practice," *American Journal of Obstetrics and Gynecology* 72 (1956): 252–259.

J. N. Martin, Jr., B. A. Harris, J. F. Huddleston, J. C. Morrison, M. G.

Propst, W. L. Wiser, H. W. Perlis, and J. T. Davidson, "Vaginal Delivery Following Previous Cesarean Birth," *American Journal of Obstetrics and Gynecology* 146 (1983): 255–263.

4. J. L. Granados, "Survey of the Management of Postterm Pregnancy," *Obstetrics and Gynecology* 63 (1984): 651–653.

D. M. F. Gibb, L. D. Cardozo, J. W. W. Studd, and D. J. Cooper, "Prolonged Pregnancy: Is Induction of Labour Indicated? A Prospective Study," *British Journal of Obstetrics and Gynaecology* 89 (1982): 292–295.

G. M. Cario, "Conservative Management of Prolonged Pregnancy Using Fetal Heart Rate Monitoring Only: A Prospective Study," *British Journal of Obstetrics and Gynaecology* 91 (1984): 31–36.

5. A. D. Murray, R. M. Dolby, R. L. Nation, and D. B. Thomas, "Effects of Epidural Anesthesia on Newborns and Their Mothers," *Child Development* 52 (1981): 71–82.

6. J. A. Read, F. C. Miller, and R. H. Paul, "Randomized Trial of Ambulation versus Oxytocin for Labor Enhancement: A Preliminary Report," *American Journal of Obstetrics and Gynecology* 139 (1981): 669–672.

7. R. P. Husemeyer, "Epidural Analgesia and Assisted Delivery," *British Journal of Obstetrics and Gynaecology* 90 (1983): 594–595.

J. W. W. Studd, J. S. Crawford, N. M. Duignan, C. J. F. Rowbotham, and A. O. Hughes, "The Effect of Lumbar Epidural Analgesia on the Rate of Cervical Dilatation and the Outcome of Labor of Spontaneous Onset," *British Journal of Obstetrics and Gynaecology* 87 (1980): 1015–1021.

E. A. Friedman, letter, *British Journal of Obstetrics and Gynaecology* 88 (1981): 464.

8. W. R. Cohen, "Influence of the Duration of Second Stage Labor on Perinatal Outcome and Puerperal Morbidity," *Obstetrics and Gynecology* 49 (1977): 266–269.

9. D. B. Stewart, "The Pelvis as a Passageway. II: The Modern Human Pelvis," *British Journal of Obstetrics and Gynaecology* 91 (1984): 618–623.

7. A PERSONAL PROTOCOL

1. The childbirth protocol given here evolved from Norma Shulman's options for childbirth.

2. J. S. Crawford, M. Burton, and P. Davies, "Time and Lateral Tilt at Cesarean Section," *British Journal of Anaesthesia* 44 (1972): 477–484.

9. HOSPITALITY

1. P. M. Butterfield, R. N. Emde, and B. B. Platt, "Effects of Silver Nitrate on Initial Visual Behavior," *American Journal of Diseases of Childhood* 132 (1978): 426.

10. GUARDIAN ANGEL OR KNIGHT ON A HIGH HORSE?

1. Frances V. Mervyn, "Communication and Joint Decision Making in Obstetrics," in *Management of Labor,* ed. W. R. Cohen and E. A. Friedman (Baltimore: University Park Press, 1983), pp. 341–353.

11. A PREGNANT PAUSE

1. J. P. Lenihan, "Relationship of Antepartum Pelvic Examinations to Premature Rupture of the Membranes," *Obstetrics and Gynecology* 83 (1984): 33–37.

2. Steen Neldham, "Fetal Movements as an Indicator of Fetal Well-Being," *Danish Medical Bulletin* 30 (1983): 274–280.

3. R. R. Lenke and J. M. Nemes, "Use of Nipple Stimulation to Obtain Contraction Stress Test," *Obstetrics and Gynecology* 63 (1984): 345–348.

   J. F. Huddleston, G. Sutliff, and D. Robinson, "Contraction Stress Test by Intermittent Nipple Stimulation," *Obstetrics and Gynecology* 63 (1984): 669–673.

4. S. Gortmaker, A. Sobol, C. Clark, D. K. Walker, and A. Geronimus, "The Survival of Very Low-Birth-Weight Infants by Level of Hospital of Birth: A Population Study of Perinatal Systems in Four States," *American Journal of Obstetrics and Gynecology,* in press.

5. G. H. Anderson, S. A. Atkinson, and M. H. Bryan, "Energy and Macronutrient Content of Human Milk during Early Lactation from Mothers Giving Birth Prematurely and at Term," *The American Journal of Clinical Nutrition* 34 (1981): 258–265.

   S. A. Atkinson, M. H. Bryan, and G. H. Anderson, "Human Milk: Differences in Nitrogen Concentration in Milk from Mothers of Term and Preterm Infants," *Journal of Pediatrics* 93 (1978): 67–69.

   S. J. Gross, R. J. David, L. Bauman, and R. M. Tomarelli, "Nutritional Composition of Milk Produced by Mothers Delivering Preterm," *Journal of Pediatrics* 96 (1980): 641–644.

S. J. Gross, R. H. Buckley, S. S. Wakil, D. C. McAllister, R. J. David, and R. G. Faix, "Elevated Ig-A Concentration in Milk Products by Mothers Delivered of Preterm Infants," *Journal of Pediatrics* 99 (1981): 389–393.

13. GETTING IT BACK TOGETHER

1. Betsy Lozoff, "Birth in Non-Industrial Societies," in *Birth, Interaction and Attachment,* ed. Marshall H. Klaus and Martha Oschrin Robertson (Skillman, N.J.: Johnson & Johnson, 1982), pp. 1–6.

INDEX

physical problems with, 14, 34, 131
psychological problems with, 29–30
rates of, 27–29, 34–35, 55, 101
reasons for, 26, 33, 34–35, 55, 60–62,
    65, 73, 81, 110–111, 112
time and, 62–65, 73, 77, 81, 113
see also legal issues; vaginal birth after
    cesarean
checkups, 114–117, 132
chemical hazards, 23
childbirth, *see* birth; labor
childbirth classes, 82, 105, 122
children
    present at birth, 90, 96, 122
    visiting after birth, 34, 93, 96
cigarettes, 23
circulation, *see* blood circulation
circumcision, 118–119
classes, *see* childbirth classes
clitoris, 49
clothing, 75, 106, 114
coaching, xi
coccyx, 10
coffee, 23
coma, 22
comfort
    in labor, 36–47, 86–87, 88–89
    in pregnancy, 114
commode, 88
communication, 6–7, 71, 93–94, 103,
    104–105, 107–108, 108–113, 124–
    129, 132
see also birth plan
complications in labor, 18, 25, 34–35, 48,
    72, 73–74, 77–78
    amniotomy as cause of, 30–31
    analgesia and anesthesia as cause of, 48–
    49, 55–56, 64
    environment as cause of, 39
    labor support and incidence of, 26–29,
    45
    medical backup for, 8, 71
    oxytocin as cause of, 31–32, 61
    see also specific problems

compression
    of baby's chest, 34
    of baby's head, 30, 32, 33
    of mother's blood vessels, 14, 15, 28,
    52
    of umbilical cord, 30
conception, 115
congenital defects, 115, 117
conscience, 5, 103, 130–131
consent, *see* informed consent
contractions
    as controlled by baby, 21–22
    in first-stage labor, 13–14
    monitoring of, 50, 51
    onset of, 11–13, 62–63
    in orgasm, 114–115
    pain of, 42–43
    postpartum, 131
    in second-stage labor, 14–17
    stimulation of, 18, 20
    in stress test, 116
    suppression of, 20
    in third-stage labor, 18
    see also labor
control, 5–6, 21–22, 39, 111
convulsions, 22
cord, *see* umbilical cord
costs, *see* fees
CPD, *see* cephalopelvic disproportion
crowning, 17, 28
cultural influences on labor, 6–7, 17, 35,
    42
C/S, *see* cesarean delivery
C-section, *see* cesarean delivery

day care, 119–120
death, *see* morbidity and mortality
defects, *see* birth defects
dehydration, 26, 63, 64, 113, 125
delivery, *see* birth; breech; cesarean deliv-
    ery; drugs; episiotomy; forceps deliv-
    ery; labor; statistics; vacuum extraction
delivery room, 90, 95, 97, 111, 128
depression postpartum, 29–30, 131

external version, 61
extraction of baby, *see* forceps delivery; vacuum extraction
eye prophylaxis, 92

failure to progress, 46, 55, 62, 64–65, 73, 81–82
family practice, 8
fasting in labor, 26, 49–50, 64, 90, 95, 111
father, *see* partner
FDA, see Food and Drug Administration
fear, *see* anxiety
feedback control, 20, 31, 57, 58
feeding, *see* bottle feeding; breast feeding
feelings, *see* psychological factors
fees
assistant's, 121
doctor's, 102, 103
hospital's, 83–84
fetal age, *see* conception; onset of labor; postmaturity; prematurity
fetal anomalies, *see* birth defects
fetal distress
amniotomy and, 30–31
cesarean delivery and, 55
intravenous fluids and, 57
in utero resuscitation for, 54
oxytocin and, 31–32
see also auscultation; electronic fetal monitoring
fetal growth, 22
fetal head, 10, 17, 26, 30, 32, 33, 38, 128
fetal heart rate, *see* auscultation; electronic fetal monitoring
fetal maturity, *see* onset of labor; postmaturity; prematurity
fetal monitoring, *see* auscultation; electronic fetal monitoring
fetal movement, 117
fetal positions, *see* anterior presentation; breech; posterior presentation; transverse presentation
fetal scalp
blood sample, 77

electrode, 50, 126
fetus
controlling labor, 11, 21–22
drugged, 23
rotation of, 38, 61
testing of, 21, 77, 116, 117
fetuscope, *see* auscultation
fever, *see* infections
"fight or flight" response, 21
films, 122, 136
financial considerations, 5, 81, 83–84, 102, 103
first stage of labor, 13–14, 62, 73, 125–126
fluids, *see* drinking in labor; edema; hydration; intravenous drip
food, *see* nutrition
Food and Drug Administration, 63
forceps delivery, 26–29, 33, 55, 60, 62, 64, 65, 77, 95, 113
frustration, *see* exhaustion; psychological factors; screaming
FTP, *see* failure to progress
furniture in childbirth, 86–87, 88–89, 123, 128

general anesthesia, 91
see also anesthesia
genetic factors, 115, 117
genitals, 122
see also circumcision; episiotomy
gestation, *see* pregnancy
glucose, *see* sugar
government agencies
state accreditation board, 91–92
see also United States government
gravity in labor, 16–18, 61
guilt, 5, 103, 130–131

hands-and-knees position, 38, 40
head, *see* fetal head
health habits, 22–24, 106, 114–115
health plan, 4–5, 124
see also fees
heart disease, 27–28, 91, 115